Norman T. Carrington MA

Brodie's Notes on Emily Brontë's

Wuthering Heights

Pan Educational London and Sydney

First published by James Brodie Ltd
This edition published 1976 by Pan Books Ltd,
Cavaye Place, London SW10 9PG
10 11 12 13 14 15 16 17 18 19 20
© James Brodie Ltd 1960
ISBN 0 330 50029 5
Printed and bound in Great Britain by
Richard Clay (The Chaucer Press) Ltd, Bungay, Suffolk

Contents

Page references are to the edition of *Wuthering Heights* published by Messrs J. M. Dent & Sons Ltd in their 'Literature of Yesterday and Today' series, as this is the edition most likely to be used in schools, but they are always accompanied by chapter references, and the Notes are planned for use with any edition of the text.

The author

In 1820 the Rev Patrick Brontë was appointed to the living of Haworth, near Keighley, in the West Riding of Yorkshire, and moved into the parsonage there. Emily was then eighteen months old.* In her *Life of Charlotte Brontë* Mrs Gaskell shows how rough, yet 'powerful in mind and body', were the people who lived there. The parsonage was a solid but not very enchanting house, standing firm against the fierce winds and driving rain which were an ally of the consumption that in due course killed all the girls of the family. From the first the Brontë children loved the moors which rose beyond the village. Emily was never so happy as when she was roaming the moorland with her dog, like her own Catherine, who wished that she were a girl again, 'half-savage, hardy and free'. She was happier alone than were her two sisters. She felt a spirit on the moors, even as Wordsworth did in the woods, a sense of a presence beyond her understanding. Like Catherine she similarly found inspiration in the moorland and loved to feel the wind over the heather when she was unable to get out. 'Do let me feel it – it comes straight down the moor – do let me have one breath!' 'I'm sure I should be myself were I once among the heather on those hills.'

The year after the move to Haworth Mrs Brontë died, and the children, who were 'grave and silent beyond their years', were thrown more and more upon their own devices. 'We were wholly dependent', says Charlotte, 'on ourselves and each other, on books and study, for the enjoyments and occupations of life'. Their aunt, Miss Branwell, came from Penzance to look after them, but, although she seems to have been a kind and dutiful woman, she showed little understanding of children. Further, she felt the change from a southern bay to a northern moor, and spent much of her time in her bedroom, for fear of catching cold. Thus the children had little companionship with her, and while they were respectful, showed her little warm affection. She taught the girls needlework and household

* She was born on 30 July 1818, at Thornton, near Bradford.

management, while their father was responsible for their other lessons. The Rev Patrick Brontë was always austere and gloomy. Like Mr Earnshaw he 'did not understand jokes from his children: he had always been strict and grave with them'. Now he had become something of an eccentric in addition. His theories on education were prompted by 'a desire to make his children hardy and indifferent to the pleasures of eating and of dress', and he brought them up in Spartan fashion. His ideas under this head may have been due to the inadequacy of his salary to bring up six children properly. Thus the Brontë children were starved of real family life.

In 1824 Charlotte and Emily became pupils at Cowan Bridge School for the Daughters of Clergymen, a school which is reproduced in Charlotte's *Jane Eyre*. After the death of their two eldest sisters, who were at school with them, they were removed, however, as the school was considered to be too damp. Back at Haworth once again, with the other two children, Branwell and Anne, they were left to make their own amusements. They were driven into a world of make-believe. They built their imaginary worlds together, and the extraordinary thing is that they put their fancies into writing. There still exist scores of tiny books, the smallest less than two inches square, in which their stories were written, and the shortage of paper resulted in such tiny hand-writing that the books can scarcely be read without a magnifying-glass. In *History of the Year 1829* Charlotte tells how the plays originated.

I will sketch the origin of our plays more explicitly if I can. First *Young Men*. Papa bought Branwell some wooden soldiers at Leeds [Mr Earnshaw's presents from Liverpool are brought to mind]; when Papa came home it was night and we were in bed, so next morning Branwell came to our door with a box of soldiers. Emily and I jumped out of bed, and I snatched up one and exclaimed, 'This is the Duke of Wellington! This shall be the Duke!' When I had said this, Emily likewise took one up and said it should be hers; when Anne came down she said one should be hers.

The twelve wooden soldiers (now become twelve young men) founded a kingdom in Africa called Great Glass Town, about which innumerable histories, 'newspapers', magazines, etc., were written by the children.

In 1831, when Charlotte went away to school again (this time at Roe Head), the four chief genii who helped the twelve, Tallii (Charlotte), Brannii (Branwell), Emmii (Emily) and Annii (Anne), decided to destroy the Great Glass Town. Charlotte wrote a poem on the event. While Charlotte was away, Emily and Anne invented another dream world, Gondal, and when she returned home she and Branwell imagined yet another kingdom, Angria, which lay to the east of Glass Town. These things are mentioned to show the active and vivid imaginations of the Brontë children. They built their play-worlds together, but Emily was the most reserved of the three girls and never spoke her inmost thoughts even to her sisters. 'My sister Emily', said Charlotte, 'was not a person of demonstrative character, nor one on the recesses of whose mind and feelings, even those nearest and dearest to her could, with impunity, intrude unlicensed'. Yet she generally took the lead and made the decisions, and she was the one most full of mischief (like Catherine). In addition to her writing of stories at an early age, Emily showed herself a gifted artist and an accomplished pianist.

On her return home Charlotte helped to educate her younger sisters until, in 1835, she returned to the school as a teacher, taking with her Emily, now a tall, attractive and imposing young lady. Emily became so homesick, however, that she had to be sent back to Haworth, and Anne came in her stead. But she too was depressed away from home, and soon returned likewise. Meanwhile Branwell, who had hoped to study painting at the Royal Academy School, had been unsuccessful in gaining admission. It was a great pity, for he was a very talented artist; indeed, his portrait of Emily is in the National Portrait Gallery. Thenceforward he tried job after job, losing each in turn.

Charlotte now had the idea of opening a school of her own, but she was warned of the great competition and at last decided to study in Brussels to equip herself more adequately. In 1842, therefore, she and Emily became pupils at the 'pensionnat' of Madame Héger. They worked hard and on the whole found the life very pleasant. Then came the news that their Aunt Branwell had died, and they had to return home. Emily decided to stay with her father, so Charlotte went back to Brussels alone. In 1844 she came back home, and again the sisters planned their school.

Once more their hopes were destroyed, however, for not long after Charlotte's return Branwell came home in disgrace from the family where he had been a tutor. Previous to this he had been dismissed by the Leeds and Manchester Railway Co. for culpable negligence as a clerk, and in his private life he had got badly into debt. It was a great shock. Their only brother, once the hope of the family, had come to this. The Brontës were a very united family, however, in trouble and in joy, and all the girls gave their spare money to pay his debts – including money that would have provided capital for the school. From then until his death in 1848 – a lingering death in which his body was fighting against drink and opium – Branwell was a constant worry to them. Charlotte, the predominantly practical and sensible one, looked for something which would help her sisters (mentally and financially) in this great trial, and eventually decided that the three of them should publish a volume of poetry. In a few months the volume appeared – *Poems by Currer, Ellis and Acton Bell* (they changed their names, but kept their initials). It was not very successful, but the trio were encouraged to go on writing and each started a novel.

In 1847 Charlotte's *Jane Eyre*, Emily's *Wuthering Heights* and Anne's *Agnes Grey* were all accepted. *Wuthering Heights* was little noticed at first, however, and its author never lived to know of its fame and her recognition as a great novelist. She died of consumption on 19 December 1848, when but thirty years of age. She triumphed over her suffering to the end and tried to appear well even when in great pain. She refused to see a doctor and came downstairs on the very day she died. 'Day by day, when I saw with what a front she met suffering, I looked on her with an anguish of wonder and love', said Charlotte. Idle though it is, one cannot help but wonder what would have been her literary achievement had she lived a life of normal length. Be that as it may, like John Bunyan she has put herself in the first rank of English storytellers by one single book.

The longest-lived of all the Brontë children was Charlotte, and she was but thirty-eight at the time of her death. Old Mr Brontë was the only healthy one of the family, and he outlived all the rest to the good old age of eighty-four.

Wuthering Heights is not autobiographical in the sense that it reproduces the *events* of the author's life, but the student will sense how it is a mirror of her experience of life, and an expression of her heart and soul. Think of the number of people in the story who die young or in the prime of life, wasting away in a lingering decline; and in the end death defeats the powerful Heathcliff when he is under forty. Emily Brontë knew how tragic life could be and spoke from her heart when she wrote this wild, haunting tragedy of two houses on the moors.

Most of the men-folk in *Wuthering Heights* are overdrawn, on the one hand frightening or boorish, on the other insipid and weak. Emily Brontë had no friends and did not mix with the villagers of Haworth.

Hence it ensued that what her mind had gathered of the real concerning them, was too exclusively confined to those tragic and terrible traits of which, in listening to the secret annals of every rude vicinage, the memory is sometimes compelled to receive the impress. Her imagination, which was a spirit more sombre than sunny, more powerful than sportive, found in such traits material whence it wrought creations like Heathcliff, like Earnshaw, like Catherine (Charlotte's Preface to the Second Edition of *Wuthering Heights*).

The only men she knew were her father and her brother, both extreme natures, the one very strict and gloomy, the other the ne'er-do-well of a good family, going downhill the faster for the help of drink and gambling – 'His golden days left long behind'.*

The similarity between Branwell and Hindley instantly springs to mind, and Branwell's ravings about his thwarted love (after he was dismissed as a tutor) may have influenced the presentation of Heathcliff in like circumstances. The characters of Heathcliff and the boy Linton, opposite extremes of strength and weakness, are the two most overdrawn, and the

* Emily's poem beginning, 'Thy sun is near meridian height'.

brutality of the one and the cowed, whining petulance of the other (another father and son of very opposite natures) appear beyond belief. The girls and women are more finely etched, and Catherine and her daughter echo the imaginative longings of their creator as she went about the tasks of the parsonage or ran out on to the moors so free. Emily Brontë is true to life in portraying the finer points of feminine behaviour, whereas the men react to powerful and obvious stimuli.

And now *Wuthering Heights* has been translated into no fewer than twenty-seven foreign tongues, including Russian and Chinese, and in our own country Haworth has become second only to Stratford-on-Avon as a place of literary pilgrimage, over sixty thousand people a year visiting the Brontë parsonage alone. There have been two plays and two films of the book, and many more plays on the Brontë family.

Students whose interest is roused to a more complete study of this remarkable family will find many books on the Brontës. One of the best for the young reader is *In the Steps of the Brontës*, by Ernest Raymond (Rich and Cowan). The facts are presented in an interesting and absorbing fashion by one who can tell a story, and, in addition, it is well illustrated by photographs. Its one weakness is that it is without illustrations of the artistic work of the Brontës and of their manuscripts, and these should be obtained from other sources.

The book

Plot

Mr Lockwood, the new tenant of Thrushcross Grange, has come to make his home in this wild moorland country in order to be free from 'the stir of society'. He finds that he has one solitary neighbour (some four miles away), Mr Heathcliff, of the strongly-built farmhouse called Wuthering Heights. After he has experienced the menacing rudeness of Mr Heathcliff and spent a terrible night in a haunted room at Wuthering Heights, his housekeeper, Mrs Dean, tells him Heathcliff's story.

Heathcliff was a gypsy-looking foundling rescued from the streets of Liverpool by Mr Earnshaw of Wuthering Heights to be brought up with his own children, Hindley and Catherine. The unwanted boy bred bad feeling in the house, and, besides Mr Earnshaw, only Catherine came to like him. Hindley especially resented the way he seemed to usurp *his* place in his father's affections.

Old Mr Earnshaw died, and when Hindley succeeded him he revenged himself on Heathcliff by making him a farm-labourer and stable-boy and subjecting him to every indignity. The only reason Heathcliff endured it was that he was passionately in love with Catherine and wanted to stay near her. She, on her side, had everything in common with him – a wild, impulsive nature and a love of the moorland heath – 'I *am* Heathcliff'. One night Heathcliff overheard her say that although she loved him intensely she had accepted a proposal of marriage from Edgar Linton, heir to the neighbouring estate, Thrushcross Grange, because a marriage with Heathcliff would degrade her. He vanished and could not be found.

Returning three years later he found Catherine married to Edgar Linton, now in possession of Thrushcross Grange. As for himself, it was obvious that he had done well. He looked a 'gentleman'. He was crafty and obtained power over Hindley, now a drunkard and a gambler, by encouraging him to gamble his inheritance away and by lending him the money to do so. All his actions were dominated by revenge. On Hindley's death he became the owner of Wuthering Heights, which was mortgaged to himself. He broke up Catherine's marriage, and indirectly caused her death upon the birth of her daughter – Cathy. He married Edgar Linton's sister Isabella (heiress to Edgar's property) and treated her abominably as a means of revenging himself on Edgar. He ill-treated Hindley's son Hareton in revenge for Hindley's treatment of him when he was young.

On the death of Edgar Linton he claimed Thrushcross Grange through his wife Isabella (Edgar's sister), who had predeceased her brother, and to make doubly sure of the inheritance he had terrorised his weakling son and Edgar's daughter into getting married just before Edgar died. His son soon died, and thus Heathcliff became the owner of Thrushcross Grange as well as Wuthering Heights (through his son if his claim through his wife was not valid). But he was not long to enjoy the succession. Death intervened once more. His own life was taken. The wheel came full circle, and the story ends with promise of marriage between Hindley's son Hareton, the real heir to Wuthering Heights, and Catherine's daughter Cathy, the real heiress to Thrushcross Grange.

The student may find the following genealogical table helpful in sorting out the family relationships.

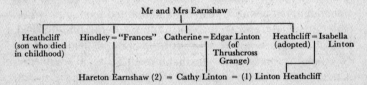

The time sequence is marked with historical exactitude, and there are only one or two slight discrepancies.

Hindley Earnshaw. *Born* 1757. *Married* 1777. *Died* Early September 1784.

Heathcliff. *b.* 'I think' 1764. *Brought to Wuthering Heights* Summer 1771. *m.* January 1784. *d.* June 1802.

Catherine Earnshaw. *b.* Late summer 1765. *m.* March 1783. *d.* 20 March 1784.

Edgar Linton. *b.* 1762. *m.* March 1783. *d.* Late August or early September 1801.

Isabella Linton. *b.* Late 1765. *m.* January 1784. *d.* Summer 1797.

Cathy Linton. *b.* 20 March 1784. *m.* (1) August 1801. (2) Arranged for 1 January 1803.

Linton Heathcliff. *b.* September 1784. *m.* August 1801. *d.* Late autumn 1801.

Hareton Earnshaw. *b.* June 1778. *m.* Arranged for 1 January 1803.

Theme

The theme of *Wuthering Heights* is a great love beside a great hatred, violent love and violent hate, consuming both parties in its course. When the lover is denied his beloved, thwarted love turns to boundless revenge. Revenge grows by what it feeds on until it becomes an overmastering mania. It should be noted, however, that it is not Heathcliff who first sets off revenge. On his father's death Hindley takes his chance to revenge himself on the outcast boy whom he hated for taking his father's affection. Heathcliff's revenge is more thorough, more violent and relentless. It is more successful, but its spirit is no worse. When one person gets the better of another, the one subdued will naturally seek to get his own back, and so a feud continues until one party is prepared to be generous and forgiving and suffer an insult or a wrong in silence. 'In taking revenge', says Francis Bacon,* 'a man is but even with his enemy; but in passing over it, he is superior'.

Heathcliff is transferred from the lower to the middle-class level of life, but he never takes to cultured ways and manners which show good breeding (except superficially). Is the theme of the story the impossibility of doing a good turn by transferring anyone from the kind of life in which he has received his early nurture? (Two modern plays deal with this problem, Shaw's *Pygmalion* and Warren Chetham-Strode's *Guinea-Pig*.) It would appear, however, that this interpretation is read into *Wuthering Heights*. There is no evidence that it was in the author's mind as she wrote. Indeed, so far as she was concerned the story had no ulterior motive or meaning behind it, posed no problems and made no attempt to ponder the imponderables. It was to be read as a story pure and simple.

* In his essay *Of Revenge*.

Construction

The story is close-packed. There are no digressions just to fill up a gap. Every incident has its place in the plot, or contributes to the feeling, or the impression of a character.

Yet the construction of *Wuthering Heights* is often regarded as its weakest point. It has been called 'clumsy' by more than one critic. The various parts contributed by Mr Lockwood, and through him by Mrs Dean, have a tendency to cut the story into segments. Putting the story into her mouth gets over certain inconveniences, however. For instance, there is no need for Emily Brontë to explain how Heathcliff made his money – she just does not happen to know.

The first three chapters are an introduction and help to set the atmosphere. Then the story turns back on itself, and, incidentally, quickens up. Even in the introductory part, however, a diary is read which goes back thirty years, and after the reading we return to the present day. The real beginning is in Chapter IV when Mr Lockwood says to his housekeeper, speaking of Heathcliff, 'Do you know anything of his history?' 'It's a cuckoo's, sir – I know all about it.' Here her words are in inverted commas. After a break in the chapter she takes over the story, and her words are no longer in inverted commas, except when she recounts her speech to people in the course of the story. So there is speech within speech, incident within incident, and occasionally the story is told at fourth hand.

At the beginning of Chapter X, when Mr Lockwood is ill for a month and Mr Heathcliff pays a call on him, the story moves forward nearly twenty years, and then back again. There is another break between Chapters XIV and XV, when Dr Kenneth comes to see Mr Lockwood.

There are incidents in the story that could not have been seen by Ellen Dean, hence Isabella's long letter (Chapter XIII), a convention from the eighteenth-century novel.

The last three chapters of the book, where Mr Lockwood unexpectedly revisits Thrushcross Grange (while still its tenant), are an addendum to the main story, a concession to popular taste, to provide the happy ending which the novel-reading public demands. In some ways, the love of Cathy and Hareton may be considered an anti-climax to the love of

Catherine and Heathcliff which dominates the book, though assuredly one would not be without it.

The opening sentences of the chapters are worth particular study, owing to their effectiveness in smoothing the transition from one event to another.

It is a mistake to condemn the structure of *Wuthering Heights* because it is different from that of other books. It must be judged on its merits in *Wuthering Heights*. The autobiographical method gives reality to a story – we are told of it by someone who saw it happen (or, in the last resort, heard it from someone who did). The use of the first person also creates suspense: there are certain things happen, and Ellen Dean does not know why, and we are kept in suspense, as she is, until she finds out. Similarly, at the beginning of the story, Mr Lockwood's interest in Heathcliff's strange household awakens the reader's interest. The book accounts for such a household. At the end we are suddenly told of Heathcliff's death, and having known him so long we cannot wait to be told how he died. But we have to, and herein is suspense created. Critics who call this clumsy need to revise their judgment. As she goes on the housekeeper interprets the events she relates and determines the reader's impression of people in the story. Whether this should be taken out of his hands is a matter of opinion – Mrs Dean is, so to speak, the official voice. Her vocabulary and her remembrance of small details over a period of thirty years are quite improbable, but in essentials there is nothing to condemn in letting the story come from her mouth (and, in most cases, her experience) or in the order in which it is told.

Reality is given to a story by the autobiographical method. We are carried along, lost in the story, and we should have to think hard if we were suddenly asked whether Mr Lockwood, his housekeeper, Heathcliff, Catherine or Isabella were telling it. The real unity of *Wuthering Heights* comes from a breathing, pulsing passion; it is a unity of feeling rather than of a preconceived plan, although it will be seen from the following paragraph that the author had a very exact and detailed plan.

The story is dated with historical accuracy (see pp.8–11). The very first chapter bears the date '1801' (see note on 'date . . Earnshaw', p.37), and the events of subsequent chapters are timed with a loving exactitude, e.g. 'one October evening', 'a fine June day', 'Easter Monday', and even 'this 20th of March'. Days are counted exactly, e.g. 'seven days glided away', '*five* nights and *four* days', 'on the fifth morning, *or rather afternoon*'. Where the time is not given by the calendar, events are placed by the season – autumn mists or winter snows, buds or blossom or whirling leaves (cf. Thomas Hardy). The effect of all this in giving a factual impression to a fictional tale is dealt with elsewhere (pp.32–33). Similarly the family trees are planned in detail.

In place the story is confined within four miles, the distance between Wuthering Heights and Thrushcross Grange, and this gives terrific concentration of effect. Even a village like Haworth has no place in the story, let alone a town like Keighley. Gimmerton is mentioned, it is true, but it is a name only; life there is out of the book.

In time, however, the story spreads over three generations, saga-like, a fashion that became popular in the twentieth century with the novels of Galsworthy and Hugh Walpole, though in their novels different generations are given different books. The unit is the family or 'house', not a single group of contemporaries.

After violent and terrifying events the book ends quietly in the manner of Shakespeare's tragedies, and with a note of hope for the future. Heathcliff and Catherine have been burnt up by their passion, but now all is over.

I lingered round them, under that benign sky; watched the moths fluttering among the heath and harebells, listened to the soft wind breathing through the grass, and wondered how any one could ever imagine unquiet slumbers for the sleepers in that quiet earth.

And after the gloom and the storm there is to be a bright sunrise on New Year's Day, when young love will start on its way again full of confidence in the future. On New Year's Day, be it noted, symbolical of the start of a new era on this bit of wind-swept heath, as in the *Idylls of the King*, after the passing of Arthur, Sir Bedivere was left as 'the new sun rose bringing the new year'.

Atmosphere and background

In spite of the happy ending, the atmosphere of *Wuthering Heights* is tragic and terrifying. The best way to see the importance of the background is to call to mind some incident in the book, and it is certain that the place where it happened will be strongly associated with the recollection and the feeling about it.

The very first chapter strikes a note of depression, which deepens with slight intermission as the book proceeds. The third shrieks with the mystery and alarm of a haunted room. We can never say that we are really happy; there is generally a shadow overhanging happiness, so that we distrust it, and it is always short-lived. The dark hatred of Heathcliff casts a cloud over everyone. There is great power and deep feeling in *Wuthering Heights*, but no sportive gaiety, save when Catherine is a child on the moors.

The events of *Wuthering Heights* have their roots in their bleak moorland setting – seldom beautiful, more often than not swept with the wind and the rain. The very title seems to show that the atmosphere of the storm-swept house was uppermost in the mind of the author as she wrote. There is scarcely an incident where the weather is not described. The student would do well to count the descriptions of beautiful scenes and those of rainy or wild ones. Rarely does a chapter begin like this, 'On the morning of a fine June day' (VIII), and the first description of a beautiful scene does not occur until Chapter X. Mist and cold, frost, wind and rain, 'gaunt thorns all stretching their limbs one way, as if craving alms of the sun', hold the scene until then, and for most of the time afterwards. Only occasionally is there a little cameo of *beautiful* description, e.g. 'There's a little flower up yonder, the last bud from the multitude of bluebells that clouded those turf steps in July with a lilac mist' (XXII. 197). Incidentally, notice that in this bleak countryside bluebells do not flower until July. (In another place – XXXII. 261 – we are told that Gimmerton is 'allas three wick after other folk' with the harvest.) Generally nature is described in the vast. These Yorkshire moors, naturally sombre and brooding, can be very beautiful at heather-time, flecked by sunshine and shadow. 'In winter', says Mr Lockwood, 'nothing more dreary, in summer nothing more divine, than those glens shut in by hills, and those bluff, bold swells of heath'. But it is the wildness of the moorland that prevails in *Wuthering Heights*. Charlotte said that the book was 'moorish, and wild, and knotty as a root of heath'. As with Cathy at Wuthering Heights, the lonely existence and lack of congenial company (outside her own family) at Haworth left its mark on Emily Brontë. Neither from Wuthering Heights nor its neighbourhood was it possible to see a single human habitation, and Ellen Dean says that in that parish 'two or three miles was the ordinary distance between cottage and cottage'. The sense of loneliness emphasizes the mysticism of the book. 'But surely you and everybody have a notion that there is or should be an existence of yours beyond you' (IX. 69). (Compare, also, Catherine's 'vague, distant look', XV. 134.) It reaches its climax in the way Catherine's spirit tortures Heathcliff for the rest of his life, and after that, it is said, their ghosts walk together on the moors. But the lonely moors equally bring the breath of life. 'Do let me feel it [the wind] – it comes straight down the moor – do let me have one breath!' (XII. 106). And in the midst of life death broods over the story (see p.vii). This, in itself, compels a powerful atmosphere of tragedy.

The happy ending comes as something of a surprise (see pp.4–5). Even there, the happiness is only a confidence in the future; the love of Hareton and Cathy had an ill beginning and a slow, hard growth. A cynical nature could find much in which they are badly suited to one another.

Sympathetic background, the way nature harmonizes with the events of the story, is dealt with under 'Style' (pp.33–34). Suffice it to say here, in a general way, that 'the atmospheric tumult' to which the station of Wuthering Heights is 'exposed in stormy weather' exactly suits the atmospheric tumult of the storms of passion in the book.

Historical and social setting
In time the story is set in the last thirty years or so of the eighteenth century, in external circumstances corresponding in essentials to the years of Emily Brontë's own life.

Wuthering Heights has been identified with a farm some

three miles from Haworth, near the village of Stanbury, but there is doubt about the exact farmstead – there are others similar scattered over the moors here and there (see note on 'WUTHERING', p.37). The farms are strongly built and are much like Wuthering Heights without and within, only much smaller (Wuthering Heights is the next best house in the neighbourhood to Thrushcross Grange – XX. 176). Some still have flagged floors and the immense old fireplaces, and, before the coming of electric power into the country recently, kept a fire burning summer and winter, as at Wuthering Heights. A casual remark (XXXII. 263) would date *Wuthering Heights* even if it were not already so exactly dated. 'As is usually the case in a coal district, a fine, red fire illuminated the chimney.' Till towards the end of the eighteenth century the common fuel at Haworth was peat, and larger houses invariably had a peat room. In Emily Brontë's time the peat room at the Brontë parsonage (no longer used) was converted into the curate's study. In the solid moorland farmhouses, with their small windows by day and their candles by night, it was often an effort to get light enough to read or write, and in the house of a 'near' master it would not be uncommon to have to read by the 'dull ray' of a 'far-off fire' (III. 17). Candles needed constant attention and could not be lit and left (see note on 'I snuffed it off', p.39). The lighting at Thrushcross Grange was brighter, and more elaborate and costly, of course, but essentially the same, a glass chandelier with tapers instead of candles. When people went to bed they took a candle up with them (or, among the wealthy, had one taken up for them), and in a farmhouse they climbed upstairs by a ladder, as if going into a loft. In many of these old Yorkshire farmhouses it is quite plain that the staircase has been added later. The inmates of these lonely houses were well guarded – by shutters, by massive bolts and bars, and by fierce dogs. The dog-kennel at Wuthering Heights is in the house (VI. 37).

Like all those who live in isolated communities the moorland folk were suspicious of strangers (see note on 'foreigners', p.41) and slow in 'thawing out'. But, as Mrs Dean observes, 'Here we are the same as anywhere else, *when you get to know us*'.

Hours of work, of course, were much longer in those days. In

Wuthering Heights servants go on as long as there is anything to do, without even a regular half-day, and all the household staff is in the field before breakfast at harvest-time. A blacksmith is willing to be knocked up to do a job after midnight.

Society was more class-conscious. Even a girl of thirteen is aware of the rigid class divisions on which life is based. 'He never said, Miss; he should have done, shouldn't he, if he's a servant?' (XVIII. 166–7). In those days servants more commonly spent their whole lives in the service of a 'house', through two or three generations, and identified themselves with its interests (for example, Mrs Dean and Joseph), instead of seeking a move to another 'place' for a shilling a week more. Of course, with limited travel facilities (none for poor folk) opportunities for moving were fewer.

At Christmas-time the village band and choir went the rounds of 'all the respectable houses', as in Thomas Hardy's *Under the Greenwood Tree*.

Dinner was at noon (it is still the mid-day meal in Yorkshire), and Mrs Dean's inability to get used to the idea of dinner at five means that Mr Lockwood has to conform to Yorkshire customs.

In the days before modern antibiotics doctors attempted to cure fevers by bleeding the patient (for which purpose leeches were still used apparently, see note on 'leeches', p.45). Illness of any kind was a long affair, and the chances of recovery correspondingly slight. Mr Lockwood has 'four weeks' torture, tossing, and sickness', and even then does not 'expect to be out of doors till spring!'. Consumption takes a heavy toll. Expectation of life is much shorter, and a woman in her mid-forties describes herself as 'elderly' (XXVIII. 239). Medical etiquette is not what it is today, and Dr Kenneth gaily talks about one patient to another on his rounds.

The chief magistrate was the local landowner, even if he was only in his early twenties. In all seriousness could a thief be threatened with the gallows (VI. 40), and public hangings are in the ordinary course of things (XVII. 153).

There was no such thing as education (in the narrow sense) unless it was individually paid for. The rich commonly engaged private tutors for their children. (Charlotte and Anne and Branwell Brontë obtained such situations.) Mr Heathcliff engages a tutor for Linton 'to come three times a week, from twenty miles distance to teach him what he pleases to learn' (XX. 178).

Horseback was the quickest way of travel, but even on horse-back fourteen miles over 'a rough road' can take three hours (XXXII. 261). A household like Thrushcross Grange has its own private carriage. Mr Earnshaw *walks* to Liverpool and back, one hundred and twenty miles, in three days (IV. 29)!

Contemporary dress is not mentioned in this survey, as a picture of it may adequately be gained from the descriptions of various characters.

Some features of the plot of *Wuthering Heights* go beyond what would be possible even at the turn of the century, for example, the forced private marriage of Cathy and Linton.

Characters

The improbabilities and coincidences which seem made to fit the plot of *Wuthering Heights* are not important. The plot is, indeed, the most unimportant part of a novel. Artistic power shows itself in characterization, and it is the men and women in a story, their human feelings in action and interaction, which have the power to make it real and lifelike. A story with a 'realistic' plot has no life if the characters are wooden, but a feeble plot becomes alive when the characters ring true. Artistic creation bears the same relation to plot as architecture to bricks and mortar.

Wuthering Heights is something more than a novel of adventure, it is a novel of character, and the characters create interest in themselves apart from their influence on the course of events. The characterization is achieved not by psychological analysis, but by descriptions of external appearances and accounts of definite deeds, so that the characters reveal themselves dramatically by their words and actions, supplemented by comments from Mrs Dean. They are not static, but in the long years covered by the novel they develop from childhood, and different characters develop in different ways. There are two key characters, and at least seven others with important parts to play, all of whom have a close connection either with

Wuthering Heights or the Grange. The contrast between the character-drawing of the women and that of the men has already been noticed on pages ix–x.

The student should make himself particularly aware of character-contrasts, which are very important in the story.

Heathcliff
'I *cannot* live without my life! I *cannot* live without my soul!'

Descriptions of Heathcliff. – As a child, IV. 30; as a boy of sixteen, VIII. 56–7; as a man, X. 78, 81; just before his death, I. 3; in death, XXXIV. 287.

Heathcliff's character is constructed on a large scale, and consideration of subtle niceties of motive is out of place. Nobody, except Catherine (and, perhaps, Hareton, in a way), likes him, nobody speaks well of him, and yet he exerts a powerful fascination on everybody.

The student must make up his mind how far Heathcliff is actively evil and how far the result of his environment and treatment as a boy. Charlotte Brontë acknowledges both influences thus. Heathcliff, she says, 'exemplifies the effects which a life of continued injustice and hard usage may produce on a naturally perverse, vindictive, and inexorable disposition'.* His revenge starts with a sense of righteous indignation; it acts on him like a drug and he needs more and more to give him the same satisfaction. Would he have had a happier life if Mr Earnshaw had left 'the poor, fatherless child' in the gutter where he found him? Certainly all the others in the story would have done.

Heathcliff is the power for evil in *Wuthering Heights*, one of those who

> in life's busy scenes immersed
> See better things and do the worst.

'A genuine bad nature', observes Mr Lockwood on the second day of his acquaintance. 'Rough as a saw-edge, and hard as whinstone', says Mrs Dean, who has known him from childhood. His character is strongly drawn. It is surprising, therefore, how little action he initiates. He arranges things so that other

---

* Letter to W. S. Williams 14 August 1848.

people work their own destruction and fall into the pit he has dug for them. He declares to Mrs Dean that he never harmed anybody – they all brought their ruin upon themselves. He is prepared to bide his time until they do so. Sullen and patient, as a child he does not reward the evil Hindley does him by good, but just endures the evil. So does he accept natural ills: 'dangerously sick' with the measles he is 'the quietest child that ever nurse watched over'. But when opportunity comes he is cunning enough to turn thrashings he has borne in silence to his own advantage, and get Hindley's pony for himself (IV. 32).

The death of Mr Earnshaw leaves him without a protector, thoroughly miserable save in one thing – his great love for Catherine, which alone makes life bearable. He is never happier than when out on the moors with her, not, it would appear, from any sharing in her love of the moorland, but simply to be with her, and the moors were the only place to which they could go. He endures life at Wuthering Heights until he finds that she considers marriage with him would degrade her. Then he stops at Wuthering Heights no longer, but suddenly goes out into the wild night. Notice that it is not just on account of his own feelings that Heathcliff goes away, it is for Catherine's sake too. Heathcliff is a villain, but there is nothing villainous about his love of Catherine. It is sincere and firm; he is neither philanderer nor adventurer. His love for her shows itself at its worst by exhibitions of bad temper (e.g. VII. 44–5, 48) when he thinks that he is in danger of losing her. A fit of bad temper is one thing, however; slow, planned, brooding revenge is another. We think of Heathcliff as a tremendous, elemental figure, but he is a nature of some variety: this giant of impulse yet has supreme powers of restraint. His turns of conduct are surprising. He throws a tureen of hot apple sauce at Edgar, but is willing to wait for a lifetime for revenge against Hindley. Locked up on Christmas Day it would have been unnatural had he not felt bitter and revengeful, but there is something horrible in his words to Mrs Dean, whatever the injury. 'I'm trying to settle how I shall pay Hindley back. I don't care how long I wait, if I can only do it at last. I hope he will not die before I do.' Heathcliff is immoderate in all things. This lingering revenge is more despicable than a sudden fierce outburst.

'This is certain', says Francis Bacon in his essay *Of Revenge*, 'that a man that studieth revenge keeps his own wounds green, which otherwise would heal and do well'. *Wuthering Heights* is the story of a man who 'keeps his own wounds green'.

How he makes his fortune in so short a time is no part of the novel, but it need not be assumed out of hand that he did it in a dishonourable way. He comes back to Wuthering Heights without any 'marks of former degradation. A half-civilised ferocity lurked yet in the depressed brows and eyes full of black fire, but it was subdued; and his manner was even dignified: quite divested of roughness, though too stern for grace'. Catherine describes him as 'a fierce, pitiless, wolfish man', but that, be it noted, is to another woman who seeks him. He wishes to do nothing to hurt Catherine. 'I wish you had sincerity enough to tell me whether Catherine would suffer greatly from his [Edgar Linton's] loss: the fear that she would restrains me.' A promise to her was always kept (XII. 104). But now that he has power and position he develops a morbid arrogance to others.

He marries Isabella 'on purpose to obtain power' over Edgar, and with diabolical ingenuity he savagely ill-treats her, cunningly keeping 'strictly within the limits of the law'. His hatred of Edgar knows no bounds, a primitive sort of hatred that would destroy every one of Edgar's family. He treats Isabella ruthlessly (e.g. XVII. 152–3). His sadistic vengeance is all the more perverse because she is not the one against whom he desires revenge. She is just a means for revenge against her brother – what she suffers in the process is of no account to him. His persecution of Linton has a purpose, the increasing of his property, but his persecution of Isabella brings him no advantage whatever – it shows a vile joy in another's misery.

After Catherine's death he is like one demented. Hearing that Catherine did not mention him at the end he bursts out,

'May she wake in torment! . . . I know that ghosts *have* wandered on earth. Be with me always – take any form – drive me mad! only *do* not leave me in this abyss, where I cannot find you!'

He dashed his head against the knotted trunk; and, lifting up his eyes, howled, not like a man, but like a savage beast.

He curses the one he claimed to love: he curses her because she had made him miserable by marrying someone else. It would therefore appear that he loves himself more than he loved her. His embittered soul sinks into itself and he again shows 'a blackness of spirit that could brood on and covet revenge for years, and deliberately prosecute its plans without a visitation of remorse'. Catherine's body is buried, but her spirit haunts him still – 'a strange way of killing! not by inches, but by fractions and hairbreadths, to beguile me with the spectre of a hope, through eighteen years!' (XXIX. 247–8). The fierce, volcanic stuff of his nature heaves and surges, and he hates with excessive violence.

His treatment of his son is comparable to that of his wife, except that he shows him no physical violence, being anxious to stretch out his days beyond those of Edgar. At his first meeting with little Linton he shows no wish to make a good impression as his father, rather the reverse, referring to the poor boy as his 'property'. Then in front of the frightened little creature he sneers, 'God! what a beauty! what a lovely, charming thing! . . . Oh, damn my soul! but that's worse than I expected – and the devil knows I was not sanguine!' After that he subdues the boy into unreasoning obedience, ultimately to make love to order, in fear of the consequences if he does not – 'It's just as if it were a task he was compelled to perform . . . for fear his father should scold him'. Heathcliff terrorises everybody. His avarice makes him care for Linton, because he is 'prospective owner of your place', and to be master of Edgar's place will satisfy his revenge. Once that has come about he cares nothing for Linton. He can die for all he cares. 'His life is not worth a farthing, and I won't spend a farthing on him.' When Linton does die and Heathcliff is master of Thrushcross Grange as well as Wuthering Heights, he is so 'near – close-handed' that he lets the better house and lives in the worse, so as not to 'miss the chance of getting a few hundreds more' (IV. 27). The possessive instinct is very strong in him. " 'I'll be *very* kind to him, you needn't fear,' he said, laughing. 'Only nobody else must be kind to him: I'm jealous of monopolizing his affection'." For this reason did he hate Edgar Linton: he regarded Catherine as *his*; he failed to get her for a wife, so no one else should enjoy her. A man – or a monster – so self-centred is unable to understand anybody else's feelings.

Young Cathy and Hareton are similarly treated with purposeless cruelty. He deprives Cathy of books just for the sake of it – he never read a book himself and had no use for books. She is kept a prisoner, and her imprisonment made more intolerable by this prohibition. But bullies like Heathcliff have a sneaking regard for people who stand up to them. Heathcliff gets his own way with sledge-hammer methods, but despises the people who give it to him. For the first time in his adult life he meets unexpected opposition. 'If you strike me, Hareton will strike you; so you may as well sit down.' Heathcliff 'seemed ready to tear Catherine in pieces', but the eyes of her mother stand out at him, and he can do no more. The memory of the first Catherine still haunts him.

'It is a poor conclusion, is it not? . . . When everything is ready and in my power, I find the will . . . has vanished. My old enemies have not beaten me; now would be the precise time to revenge myself on their representatives: I could do it; and none could hinder me. But where is the use? I don't care for striking . . . I have lost the faculty of enjoying their destruction, and I am too idle to destroy for nothing.'

He sees Cathy in Hareton, too, and refers to 'the constant torment' he suffers.

'His startling likeness to Catherine connected him fearfully with her. . . . What is not connected with her to me? and what does not recall her? I cannot look down to this floor, but her features are shaped in the flags! In every cloud, in every tree – filling the air at night, and caught by glimpses in every object by day – I am surrounded with her image! . . . Well, Hareton's aspect was the ghost of my immortal love.'

And so he is made 'regardless' how Hareton and his cousin 'go on together'. He gets even 'fonder of continued solitude, and perhaps still more laconic in company'. 'O God!' he exclaims. 'It is a long fight, I wish it were over!'

Just before his death, Heathcliff is in a queer, unearthly happiness – '*very much* excited, and wild and glad!' staring as if he saw 'an unearthly vision'. 'I'm too happy,' he says; 'and yet I'm not happy enough. My soul's bliss kills my body, but does not satisfy itself!' He goes out on midnight excursions and paces the room when he returns, muttering Catherine's name. It was in her bed that he died, with a 'frightful, life-like gaze of exultation on his face', and a sneer on his lips. The doctor could assign no physical cause for his death. He was buried 'as he had wished' (see XXIX. 246 and XXXIV. 279) 'to the scandal of the whole neighbourhood'. But on rainy nights his ghost walks abroad, they say; indeed, there are those who swear that they have seen the 'two on 'em'.

Catherine Earnshaw
'I *am* Heathcliff.'

Descriptions of Catherine. – As a child, V. 34; as a girl of fourteen, VII. 43; pale and ill, XV. 133–4; in death, XVI. 141.

Catherine is a regular tomboy, an open-air girl, 'a wild, hatless little savage' running barefoot over the moors. Before she was six years old she could 'ride any horse in the stable'. Bonny, carefree, capricious, impetuous, a little minx, she really 'meant no harm' and is good at heart. She naturally takes the lead and likes to play at being mistress. Only by 'art', not force, is it possible to control her. She does not flinch at danger, and when caught by the Linton's bulldog, 'She did not yell out – no! she would have scorned to do it', and she urged Heathcliff to save himself and leave her.

After sharing the culture of the Linton home for five weeks she is a different girl. She is now fourteen and has taken readily to 'fine clothes and flattery' and has become 'very dignified', 'quite a beauty'. Heathcliff and she are still constant companions, but she can be selfish and unthinking in her words before him. Heathcliff is unchanging; she is unpredictable. She wants to be popular, and so develops a 'double character', polite and agreeable at the Linton's, 'but at home she had small inclination to practise politeness that would only be laughed at, and restrain an unruly nature when it would bring her neither credit nor praise'. Her 'dreadfully wayward' nature, her 'falsehood and violence' threaten to lose her Edgar Linton (VIII. 59–61). Heathcliff, too, has a bad temper, but he does not try to find excuses to justify himself – the resort of a weaker (or feminine?) nature. Her ambition makes her want to keep Edgar, so, in truly feminine fashion, she retrieves the situation by tears; he proposes before he goes and she accompanies him. Heathcliff has her heart; she has agreed to marry Edgar for his position. She feels uneasy about it, and therefore petulantly asks Nelly whether she has done wrong. Not that she wants Nelly's frank opinion; she wants Nelly to agree with her, to lend her support to a decision she knows in her heart of hearts to be wrong. How much she knows it to be wrong is revealed as her conversation with Nelly continues –

'I've no more business to marry Edgar Linton that I have to be in heaven; and if the wicked man in there had not brought Heathcliff so low, I shouldn't have thought of it. It would degrade me to marry Heathcliff now; so he shall never know how I love him: and that, not because he's handsome, Nelly, but because he's more myself than I am. Whatever our souls are made of, his and mine are the same; and Linton's is as different as a moonbeam from lightning, or frost from fire.'

It is futile to conjecture whether she would still have married Linton had she found Heathcliff that night in the storm.

As a patient she is 'wearisome and headstrong as a patient could be', very different from Heathcliff (see p.13), and after recovery 'saucier and more passionate, and haughtier than ever'. She gets thoroughly spoilt, as the doctor says that she must have her own way, and she trades on her illness and gets everything she wants by 'raging'. She knows the power of her anger and makes full use of it (XI. 100). Always 'she felt small trouble regarding any subject, save her own concerns', and now she therefore becomes more and more self-willed and self-centred. When Edgar does not wish to talk in the middle of the night, she goes to Ellen's room and pulls her by the hair so that she can wake up and talk (or listen) to her instead. In her conversation she runs down her husband – referring to him as 'that creature', as if he should be expected to welcome his wife's former lover into his home. She considers herself 'an angel' as she goes to make her peace with Edgar, but soon afterwards she shows herself a devil in her malicious delight in petty-minded discomfiture of Isabella in front of Heathcliff. She is capable of more self-control than she would have people believe; Mrs

Dean thinks that 'a person who could plan the turning of her fits of passion to account, beforehand, might by exerting her will, manage to control herself tolerably, even while under their influence', and her husband is convinced that she 'can be as stoical as anyone', when she pleases.

Edgar puts the choice before her: she must give up Heathcliff or give up him. But she refuses to be bound. 'She's hard to guide any way but her own.' She takes refuge in her illness again – 'Don't you see I can scarcely stand?' A theatrical starving act becomes a real illness, which leaves 'our fiery Catherine . . . no better than a wailing child'. 'A stout, hearty lass like Catherine, does not fall ill for a trifle.' It is what she has on her mind that causes her delirium – and her listlessness. She has given her body to Linton, but Heathcliff has her soul. She pays the price. She has only herself to blame. So her life goes out as little Cathy's begins.

Out of life she goes, but not out of the story. So far as Heathcliff is concerned she is mightier in death than in life, her presence pursuing him in the more terrible world of the supernatural and making him 'the sport' of an 'intolerable torture' (see p.15). Her influence after death is grim and sardonic, very different from that of the bright, wilful creature whom he knew at first. 'Infernal', Heathcliff calls it. 'She showed herself,' he says, 'as she often was in life, a devil to me.' Or is it that her influence affects his morose nature in this way?

Whatever the reader may think of Catherine and of Heathcliff, however, certain it is that he cannot help being fascinated by both.

Cathy* Linton
'She's a beauty, it is true; but not an angel.'

Descriptions of Cathy. – As a child of twelve, XVIII. 161–2; as a girl of sixteen, XXI. 182 and 185; as a young widow, a year later, II. 8; as a young lady of nineteen, XXXII. 263; compared with Hareton, XXXIII. 276.

---

* Mr Linton's use of this diminutive to distinguish her from her mother is observed generally in these Notes for clarity in allusion (see XVII. 157).

When Catherine dies her daughter immediately takes her place in the reader's interest – 'The most winning thing that ever brought sunshine into a desolate house'. Young Cathy Linton is a weaker creature than Catherine Earnshaw, combining her father's 'soft and mild' nature with her mother's headstrong caprice. She is vivacious, without being tempestuous. The qualities she inherits from either are given at the beginning of Chapter XVIII. None the less she is a spoilt, molly-coddled child, never let out of the company of adults, never mixing with children of her own age, brought up over-carefully by an anxious father. (How different from the upbringing of her mother, allowed to roam over the moors at will!) She is always chattering and 'worrying', asking awkward questions (as children do), she cannot be still a minute, and at thirteen is a very trying child. When she fails to get her own way with Ellen Dean she gets peevish, but she accepts her father's judgment as of more authority. She can be as proud and wilful as her mother, and like her knows how to bear down opposition with a woman's weapons – in her case heavy eyes and falling tears (cf. pp.18–9).

Naturally an intelligent girl who 'had not once been beyond the range of the park by herself', and little farther accompanied wonders what lies beyond the horizon. She feels the pull of the 'top of those hills'. Like all children she desires what is forbidden all the more, and she manages to elude her guardian in her father's absence from home. It is thus that she meets Hareton. Incidentally Mrs Dean records that Cathy promised not to tell her father where she had been, and that she kept the promise faithfully.

Little wonder that a solitary child like this looks forward to having a cousin of her own age to live with her and indulges 'most sanguine anticipations' of his innumerable excellences. But her 'high glee' is soon turned to 'passionate tears' as he leaves the Grange for an unknown destination.

Then, after three years, she finds that, unknown to her, all the time he has been at the next farmstead. Her marriage with him is the most incredible part of the plot. As support for the story we may remember that no sooner had Cathy welcomed her unknown cousin that he had been snatched away from her. Linton and Hareton were the only boys to whom she had talked by the time she was sixteen, and Hareton appeared to her as an uncouth servant – certainly not as a 'real' cousin. She was tender-hearted by nature and was sorry for Linton. Heathcliff well calculated how to appeal to her. Had she not heard him say, 'He'll be under the sod before summer, unless you restore him?' Who could refuse such an appeal? The sending of love-letters by the milk-boy was a romantic contrivance which would lend glamour to a prohibited association. Whatever allowances are made, however, it is difficult to believe that a girl of her spirit would have consented to marry Linton under compulsion, as the result of getting caught in a cunning trap, even at the cost of being away from her father in his last hours. It is asking too much to believe that a girl could be forced into such a marriage (see p.11). It is, indeed, difficult to imagine her marrying such a boy under any circumstances.

Where Cathy loves and is accepted she is warm-hearted and considerate; no one could have nursed a dying father more tenderly. She shows extreme patience with Linton. But where she is just tolerated she stands on her dignity and can be 'as chill as an icicle, and as high as a princess'. 'I despise you,' she says, 'and will have nothing to say to any of you. When I would have given my life for one kind word, even to see one of your faces, you all kept off.' So, as time goes on, her heart gets cold and subdues itself to what it works in, and she becomes as rude as the 'clowns and misanthropists' with whom she lives, without a kind word to anybody. Very lonely, she prefers 'quarrelling with Joseph in the kitchen to setting at peace in her solitude'. Her degradation of character becomes pathetic.

It is the attempt to win her other cousin, Hareton, as a lover that gives her something to live for and brings back to her face the smiles that Mr Lockwood found so irresistible. 'I must show him some way that I like him – that I want to be friends' (XXII. 269). It takes her some time to find a way – between perversity and winsomeness. Not the least effective trick to make him declare himself is her defiance of Heathcliff, followed by an appeal to Hareton to champion a lady in distress. (This is the best example of her mother's spirit.) Of course, neither knows anything of the effect of two pairs of the Earnshaw's dark eyes on Heathcliff. The incident arises out of Cathy's plans for a pretty garden. She shares her mother's liking for the open air and her father's preference for indoor pursuits. She likes a garden and at the same time she finds life without books unbearable.

An attractive girl, after all, but a character lacking her mother's fire and force. Inspiration takes charge of her mother, she is driven like the wind on the heath, and the emotional achievement is titanic. There is a strangeness linking her with outside forces, which she cannot comprehend, much less control. Cathy's lack of this compelling power is not mentioned in censure of the author, rather the reverse. If Cathy rose to the heights of Catherine, the second half of the novel would be an anticlimax, and the dominance of Catherine over the whole conception weakened. The book would be broken-backed and would divide into two separate halves. Cathy is a prose Catherine, more of the stuff of ordinary life, and easier for a man to live with from day to day. Thus, at the end of the book, when the two rival houses are to be joined, we are left with a deep feeling that the future looks better and brighter, in spite of the suggestion of cold reason that it would not have been difficult to find a man more suited to be her husband had her choice been wider (see p.8). Remember that it was she who did the choosing. Hareton was attracted to her at first, but her subsequent treatment of him had alienated him.

Edgar Linton
Kind, and trustful, and honourable.

Descriptions of Edgar. – VII. 47, and of his portrait, VIII. 55.
Edgar Linton is well-intentioned, but weak (the opposite of Heathcliff, who is ill-intentioned and strong). This is an estimate of his character, of course, and not a censure of the author's drawing of it, for beside Catherine and Heathcliff he is meant to be weak. His physique sorts with his character – he is only half as broad across the shoulders as Heathcliff. He is a typical Linton. The Lintons, generally, are fair and good-

looking, with big blue eyes and small features, delicate and well-mannered, conscious of their gentility and anxious to be respectable.

As a boy he is timid and 'stands gaping at a distance' among the excitement of Catherine's capture and introduction to the house. He can use his tongue, however, and as a visitor at Wuthering Heights he is not above trying to make Heathcliff look small, and telling a lie about it into the bargain (VII. 48–9. Cf. Catherine, VIII. 59).

So far as he is concerned, there is nothing to show that his marriage to Catherine was a mistake. Catherine and he 'were really in possession of deep and growing happiness', and *had Heathcliff never returned* there was no reason why they should not have continued so. It would perhaps have been better had he forbidden Heathcliff the house at once, instead of indulging his wife's fancy, but it is easy to be wise after the event. He is in a very difficult position. He lacks directive and puts off making a decision. When it comes to the point and Heathcliff is turned out, Edgar cuts a very sorry figure beside him, and Heathcliff has the honours of the encounter.

He similarly loses our respect when he lets his wife's tongue bring him to tears, but he very wisely gives her her fling when she shuts herself in her room and hopes that everyone will be most worried about her. There is comfort enough to be found with his books. He likes a quiet life. But when Catherine turns out to be really ill he is full of self-reproach.

He does not show the same willingness to forgive and forget with Isabella as he does with his wife, however. Once she has left his home he has finished with her. None the less he is determined to do the best for her boy, and under the circumstances acts wisely and kindly on the one night he stays at the Grange.

His daughter is the apple of his eye, all that is left to him, and whatever our opinion of her upbringing (see p.20) we cannot doubt that he does his very best for her according to his own lights. And, after all, he has very particular and very sound reasons for not wishing her to go to Wuthering Heights.

His procrastination in altering his will costs his daughter her inheritance, but, as it turns out, gains her a better husband *and* the inheritance.

Isabella

'My heart returned to Thrushcross Grange in twenty-four hours after I left it.'

Descriptions of Isabella. – As a young lady of eighteen, X. 83 and 85; as Mrs Heathcliff, XVII. 145–6.

Brother and sister have much in common. Isabella does not make a deep impression, she is more acted upon than acting. Everyone in the household likes her. She is a well-bred young lady, but weak and sometimes peevish. She is not an out-of-door girl like Catherine. Living in seclusion, it is not surprising that she should try to win the only presentable man calling at the Grange and gain (as she thinks) the status and independence of a married woman, instead of living on sufferance as a poor relation in her brother's establishment. She resents the way that Catherine tries to exclude her from Heathcliff's company. The opposition of her brother and Catherine to her one-sided romance adds determination to her pursuit of Heathcliff. Catherine completely loses control of herself at the thought of another woman enjoying Heathcliff, and is very spiteful to Isabella in and out of Heathcliff's company (X. 86–90). Meanwhile Isabella pines and mopes. But her mind is made up; she is wilfully blind to the evidence, and elopes, hoping for the best in spite of all. She has no knowledge of Heathcliff's real reason for marrying her. Her marriage turns to dust and ashes as soon as she is back from her honeymoon, and she runs away from Wuthering Heights within a fortnight.

Even the child she gains from her marriage with Heathcliff turns out to be, *in its mother's view*, a 'peevish creature'. Mothers are not prone to advertise their children's failings in this way, and it makes us wonder whether Linton's disposition may not have derived in some measure from an unsympathetic mother.

Linton Heathcliff

'The worst-tempered bit of a sickly slip that ever struggled into its teens.'

Descriptions of Linton. – As a boy of twelve, XIX. 171 (compared with Edgar Linton); at sixteen, XXI. 185.

This puny, snivelling, sorry creature of a boy is at the best to be pitied, at the worst to be despised. A 'peevish creature' to begin with, under Heathcliff the poor boy grew up in 'utter lack of sympathy' and knew that he was reared for an ulterior purpose and not for love of himself. He was 'kept', not brought up.

Add to this a constitution that hung on a thread – he was 'constantly getting coughs, and colds, and aches, and pains of some sort' – and it will be seen that the 'pitiful lath of a crater' was miserable enough. He retained some grace of manner that told of a cultured early upbringing with his mother, beside a Heathcliff-like strain which, fortunately, he had no power to indulge – 'I hope you'll die in a garret! starved to death'.

Like Catherine he makes the most of illness to get other people's attention and complaisance, but in a snivelling and despicable way.

He sighed and moaned like one under great suffering, and kept it up for a quarter of an hour; on purpose to distress his cousin apparently, for whenever he caught a stifled sob from her he put renewed pain and pathos into the inflections of his voice.

And he began to wail aloud, for very pity of himself.

Catherine's self-pity was a ruse to get what she wanted. Linton's serves the same purpose, but it is a real self-pity.

When Cathy tries to help Linton he is most perverse and provocative. First of all his pillow is not high enough; then it is too high. What a miserable, selfish, make-believe sort of a lover it is who complains of having to write love-letters and who says, 'Don't kiss me: it takes my breath'! Cathy has taken the trouble to come to see him, and the only thanks he can give is, 'I was not as ill when you entered, as I am at present – was I?' He takes everything anyone does for him for granted.

He is no sport, and at sixteen years of age cannot bear to lose a game – even to a girl. He and Cathy are little suited to one another. 'He wanted all to lie in an ecstasy of peace; I wanted all to sparkle and dance in a glorious jubilee.' When Cathy goes to see him she never knows which way his 'unhappy temper' will turn, and has only three happy evenings with him in three weeks, 'now with his selfishness and spite, and now with his sufferings'. As he becomes worse he regards 'the good-humoured mirth of others as an insult'.

But he is never sincere, acting on his own behalf. He makes love under orders, terrorised by his father, 'up in alarm for his dear self'. 'Oh! darling Catherine! you mustn't go and leave me, after all. You *must* obey my father – you *must*.' His mortal terror of Heathcliff gives the boy 'his coward's eloquence'. After she has married him Cathy says that she knows he loves her, but there is no evidence of it in the story.

When his life is snuffed out we are inclined to agree with Heathcliff that it is not worth a farthing, and to be glad that our bright Cathy is not to be condemned to a life with him. There is not a single thing about him that we can admire. The pity we feel for him is not pity for patient suffering, but the sort of pity we should feel for a worm upon which we happened to tread in the garden. He has served his purpose for Heathcliff, and for the plot of the novel, by dying at the right time to bring Cathy's inheritance into his father's possession.

Hareton Earnshaw
'Hareton, with all his bashfulness, isn't a model of nice behaviour.'

Descriptions of Hareton. – At eighteen, XVIII. 168; as a young man, II. 8.

The Earnshaw family are spirited, impulsive and strong-willed. Cathy has these qualities in a polite, well-bred nature, Hareton shows them in a rough, unmannerly brute.

Nowadays, when it is fashionable to make parents or 'environment' responsible for children's misbehaviour, much attention would have been directed to the hideous treatment he received from a drunken father and the subconscious 'complex' this produced. With such a father he became devoted to Heathcliff, who had, indeed, saved his life, and who says (with a purpose) that he 'mun do as he will'. Any child likes a man who tells him he can do what he likes. After his father is dead he looks up to Heathcliff without knowing how he has seized his inheritance. Heathcliff did not treat him physically ill, owing to 'his fearless nature': it was the timid whom Heathcliff liked to oppress (see pp.14–15). Hareton has no fear of adults and as a young child he slings stones at enquirers at the gate, and is encouraged to do so. When Isabella tries to make friends with him he threatens to set the bulldog on her. He shows no finer feelings and hangs a litter of puppies on a chair-back without compunction – at least, no comment is made on his attitude to such a distasteful task by Isabella, who mentions it. This is a macabre touch and leaves an impression hardly dispelled by his subsequent improvement. He is not reproved for bad language. He is a boy after Heathcliff's own heart. Heathcliff deliberately tries to bring him up like a boor, to make him 'scorn everything extra-animal as silly and weak'. Poor Hareton knows no better.

But Ellen thought she could detect in his face 'a mind own-ing better qualities than his father ever possessed'. Heathcliff speaks of him as 'gold put to the use of paving-stones'. Cathy likes him – till she assumes him to be a servant. He has his pride and flares up at her mistake, but his anger does not last long, and he is soon moved by Cathy's distress and tries to make his peace with her (XVIII. 168).

Naturally such a rough, strong type cannot put up with Linton's peevish snivelling, and Hareton makes Linton a standing jest. Part of his animosity to Linton is because *he* likes Cathy, too. Laughed at for being a dunce, he tries hard – and with no encouragement – to teach himself to read so that he will stand better in her opinion. After Linton's death he tries to help Cathy in his own awkward way, until she silences him with words of contempt. Later, to his chagrin, she makes fun of his efforts to read in front of Mr Lockwood, and is indeed a 'little wretch'. A slap – 'a physical argument' – is the only answer he knows for such an attack, and for a long time he is 'sullen and silent' in her presence.

' I shall have naught to do wi' you and your mucky pride, and your damned mocking tricks!' he answered. 'I'll go to hell, body and soul, before I look sideways after you again. Side out o' t' gait, now; this minute!'

But he bears no lasting resentment when he sees that she is really anxious to put things right between them, and (though not immediately) he grasps the hand put out to help him. His warm heart glows under her growing interest in him. He needs the companionship of a woman to give him grace. 'He had been content with daily labour and rough animal enjoyments till Catherine crossed his path.' Now a reading lesson becomes a double joy. For the first time in his life Hareton shows himself ready to brave Heathcliff – at her behest. 'Together they would brave Satan and all his legions.' And, surely, if Hareton had been true to Heathcliff, he would find it easier and more rewarding to be true to her, with all her faults.

Joseph

It was his vocation to be where he had plenty of wickedness to reprove.

A short description of Joseph, I. 2.

Joseph parades his religion with a pharisaic holier-than-thou sense of superiority; but in his heart there is no humanity, no understanding, no charity, no tolerance. He is 'the wearisomest self-righteous Pharisee that ever ransacked a Bible to rake the promises to himself and fling the curses on his neighbours'. 'Thank Hiven for all!' he says. 'All warks togither for gooid to them as iz chozzen, and piked out fro' th' rubbidge!' He makes religion repellent. He knows the words of the Bible, but has none of the spirit of Christianity. He interprets everyone's actions in the worst light, and his croaking voice suits his unending complaints. He is always on the watch for an opportunity 'to thrust in his evil tongue'. The most avowedly religious person in the book is the most spiteful, and whatever he has to say is put in the most provocative way possible. He cannot take a message without delivering it in a defiantly arrogant manner (XIX. 173–4). The man who talks most of heaven is the most earthy, and 'an old cynic' into the bargain. In spite of all his talk, in essentials he leads an animal existence. When he is dressed in his Sunday suit his 'most sanctimonious and sourest face' is all the more noticeable. His laughter is derisive, always at someone's expense, as when he first sees young Linton and sneers, 'He's swopped wi' ye, maister, an' yon's his lass!' As soon as his master's back is turned the man 'piked out fro' th' rubbidge' sits down 'beside a roaring fire, a quart of ale on the table near him', and is deaf to all calls to work.

But even this self-righteous old Pharisee has *one* real loyalty. He is not just a Dickensian caricature of a hypocrite. He has fixed notions of inheritance: he knows who is 'the rightful heir' to the farm, and he never forgets it, showing a 'narrow-minded partiality which prompted him to flatter and pet him [Hareton], as a boy, because he was the head of the old family'. People in life are not all good or all bad, but made up of complex motives, and this good point in his character makes him more human. There is another: 'Joseph is an old rascal,' says Ellen Dean, 'but no liar.' Joseph's self-conceit is tremendous, and in his own eyes he is the only righteous man alive, but he never tries to make capital for himself out of Heathcliff's usurpation, and condemns it, if only in muttered asides. Joseph is a family servant, loyal at heart to the family whom he served in the beginning.

Joseph's dour dialect speech, which provides a contrast to the love-making scenes, does much to give local colour to the narrative. Joseph has no part in the plot, but serves for background, a fitting servant for Heathcliff (although he hates him), an able guardian of his door against strangers and preserver of the barren atmosphere of his house.

Mrs Dean

I went about my household duties, convinced that the Grange had but one sensible soul in its walls, and that lodged in my body.

Mrs Dean is a connecting-link who comes into contact with all the characters. In some novels the characters have a common meeting ground (e.g. the choir in *Under the Greenwood Tree*, or the Rainbow Inn in *Silas Marner*); here Mrs Dean goes the round of the various characters or they come and talk to her. 'A matronly lady', she gets the title 'Mrs' ('Mistress Dean') from the importance of her situation – quite usual in those days.

Like Joseph she is another faithful family servant, 'taken as a fixture along with the house', and unwilling to change to new-fangled notions (such as dinner at five) for any fresh employer. These are the only ways in which she resembles Joseph. Unlike Joseph she combines conscientiousness in her duties with kindness of disposition, and she is invaluable as a nurse in sickness, of which there is much in the book. The ordering of the affairs of a great house demands many duties and a certain presence, and at Thrushcross Grange only once does anyone complain of Mrs Dean's management of affairs (Mr Linton, XII. 109), except the girls when they are in a pet. She is called to do anything from sending to the village for some oranges to being a mother to a motherless child. One of her duties turns out to be telling the story of Wuthering Heights, and to please her master she is willing to sit up into the early hours to do so. Mr Lockwood tells the story 'in her own words, only a little condensed. She is, on the whole, a very fair narrator, and I don't think I could improve on her style'. She has, she says, read more than one would think. But she is not a subservient vassal who holds her tongue when she thinks that wrong is being done, and she rightly calls Hindley 'worse than a heathen' for his treatment of his boy or speaks up and tells Catherine when she is mistaken (X. 83). But in their absence she dutifully defends the members of the family before others. Such trusty family servants completely respect the confidences of their master or mistress, and are appealed to for advice rather than the family, for the housekeeper cannot laugh at their inmost secrets and will not reveal them to all and sundry. Her simple, common-sense advice stands out against the passionate, wayward impulses of some of those whom she serves. Like her mother, a 'canty dame' indeed.

It is, therefore, all the more surprising to find her opening *and reading* Cathy's 'copious love-letters'. Most mothers, let alone housekeepers, would never think of such an intrusion into the private affairs of their teen-age daughters. 'Worthy Mrs Dean, I like you, but I don't like your double-dealing', says Heathcliff – unjustly, but in this case it might be allowed to be a just comment. Furthermore, was she doing her duty to Mr Linton by letting Heathcliff into his house behind his back (XV. 133–5, XVI. 144), and getting the other servants out of the way so that she could do it secretly? Similarly she promised Cathy to keep certain things from her father. Conversely she was doing a very unwise thing to place herself in Cathy's power by making Cathy promise not to tell her father that she had been to Wuthering Heights (XVIII. 170). They were thus in a position to blackmail one another.

A housekeeper and a mistress, but beneath the externals of position is a lasting affection and understanding between them. When she is wanted at Wuthering Heights, Ellen Dean cannot rest at Thrushcross Grange, and she risks life in Heathcliff's frightening household to be where she is needed. 'I obeyed joy-fully', she says, 'for Catherine's sake', leaving an inferior sub-stitute to do the job that Mr Lockwood was paying her to do, without his permission or knowledge. An easier post, higher wages – nothing would have tempted her to leave 'her' family. 'The crown of all her wishes' is not a better position, indeed nothing for herself, but 'the union of those two. I shall envy no one on their wedding-day: there won't be a happier woman than myself in England!' Her heart is in her work as such, not in her pocket.

Her attitude to life is the conventionally proper and respectable one. In a world of ghosts and raving loves and hat-reds she stands for common sense, and, conversely, such out-landish incidents seem more credible because she is concerned in them.

It says much for the author's power of characterization that Mrs Dean, who is really only a medium to get the story across, has so much distinctive personal character.

Style

The most important quality of the style is its naturalness. A well but not conventionally educated girl has achieved great-ness by 'letting herself go'. Her style is not modelled on anyone else; she is just being herself. In its beauty and in its fire the style is easy and spontaneous. There is no bombast, no straining after effect. The prose is not over-written – there is no elabora-tion for its own sake, merely to create an impression on the reader.

This straightforward style sometimes bounds or swells with a rhythmic quality (e.g. XIV. 136, III. 20, XII. 108, XIII. 115, XVI. 142), not a regular rhythm like the rhythm of poetry but a rhythm like the waves of the sea, in continuous motion yet never exactly the same. Like the poet she was, Emily uses words with a rhythm and beauty that echo the sense and the feeling.

The style is varied to suit the theme. It can be swift and force-ful, for example, the scene where Heathcliff meets Catherine at Thrushcross Grange while Edgar is at church (XV. 136–40), or where he describes how he opened Catherine's coffin (XXIX.

247–48). These descriptions have a convulsive quiver, and their tenseness is sustained for a long time. In such passages the short sentences help the effect of eagerness and excitement. On the contrary the style can be slow and restful, as in the closing sentence of the novel. *Wuthering Heights* is not entirely violent and rapid. The style is strong and at the same time supple. Short sentences can give excitement and suspense to a still picture, for example, the description of Heathcliff in death (XXXIV. 287). The pathos of *Wuthering Heights* truly goes to the heart, as indeed it is *from* the heart, for instance, in the description of Catherine's delirium (XII. 104–108), here again sustained over several pages. The speech of Joseph in racy Yorkshire dialect gives a wiry vigour to the scenes where it is appropriate.

Whether outdoors or indoors Emily Brontë's descriptions sound authentic, not conventional. They are true and clear and vivid, and beautifully described with the touch of an artist. There are so many descriptions of nature that particular reference would be misleading. The details of these are well-chosen and they are not overloaded. The description of the valley of Gimmerton with a long line of mist over it (X. 79), and of the 'fresh watery afternoon' 'boding abundant rain' (XXII. 196), take only a few lines but are wonderfully clear. The wide sweep of moorland is what seems most to appeal to Emily Brontë, and she gives herself much opportunity for landscape painting, as a great deal of the action takes place out of doors (see pp.7–8). There is a rare touch of pathos in Catherine's fanciful description as she plucks a lapwing's feather from her pillow in her delirium (XI. 104). Emily Brontë's descriptions not only appeal to the sense of sight, the sense to which authors most commonly appeal, but to the sense of sound as well, for example, the beautiful description of the music of the beck contrasted with that of the summer leaves (XV. 134).

The description of the family sitting-room at Wuthering Heights is an example of a description that is over-loaded. The illusion of reality would be better achieved by cutting. Such a description is not dramatic in so far as it gives more than the eye would normally take in at the time. In real life we should notice one or two things that stood out, and as we paid further visits to the house we should become aware of the details. This is the usual method of description in a modern novel. Selection is a fundamental principle in all art – the power to spot the thing that matters. It is not the *amount* of detail that makes a picture vivid, but the *significance* of the detail selected. Mere accumulation of detail only confuses the impression. Incidentally, the reader would do well to notice the light and shade in this description, which have the effect of relieving it, and in other descriptions, too, for there is not much colour in the book – indeed, it would not be appropriate.

A sense of reality is given to the story by little circumstantial details, given almost (it seems) by accident. They help to give clearer definition to the picture in the reader's mind, and when such details are 'remembered' by the narrator it seems to give all the reality of fact to fiction. 'I saw a pair of ousels passing and repassing *scarcely three feet from him*' (XVI. 142). 'I knocked over Hareton, who was hanging a litter of puppies *from a chair-back in the doorway*' (XVII. 156). (Was this something Emily Brontë had seen among the rough Haworth folk?) The details in the time sequence, the season and the weather (see p.6) are the best illustration of circumstantial detail. Sometimes a mistake adds a sense of truthfulness in relation, for we are all forgetful.

'You have lived here a considerable time,' I commenced; 'did you not say sixteen years?'
'Eighteen, sir.'

Even Mrs Dean, of prodigious memory, has her uncertain moments – 'They call the Methodists' or Baptists' place (I can't say which it is), at Gimmerton, a chapel'. Her very uncertainty makes her story sound more true.

The purpose of many nature descriptions is to create sympathetic background for the events of the story (see p.8). Ghosts walk on rainy nights (XXXIV. 288) and hover round the windows in a shivering snow-storm (III. 20–22). The stormy night when Mr Earnshaw died (V. 35–36) contrasts with the fine June morning when his grandson is born (VIII. 53); there is a terrific thunderstorm on the night that Heathcliff rushes out from Wuthering Heights with a storm in his soul (IX. 71–72); Isabella's desperate escape to a miserable married life takes place on a pitch black night (XII. 107–108), her escape from it after being stabbed with a dinner knife is through driving sleet and snow; Cathy's happy birthday outing is favoured with a 'beautiful spring day' (XXI. 182), but when she goes out sadly the afternoon 'bodes abundant rain' (XXII. 196). When 'Catherine's heart was clouded now in double darkness (XXII. 201), 'the rain began to drive through the moaning branches of the trees'. Heathcliff dies on a night of wind and pouring rain, when the lattice flaps to and fro, but on the evening when Mr Lockwood finds Cathy and Hareton making love over a reading lesson, it is 'sweet, warm weather' and 'a fragrance of stocks and wallflowers wafted on the air from amongst the homely fruit-trees' (XXXII. 261 and 263), and symbolically enough the setting sun is giving way to a splendid moon. And when the tumult is over, as he walks homeward Mr Lockwood lingers round the quiet tombstones under a 'benign sky', described in a passage of sublime beauty.

There is much conversation in the story, which gives a dramatic effect, but the conversation (save Joseph's) often lacks spontaneity. All the characters – children and grown-ups alike – speak in much the same vocabulary (except in moments of excitement), a rather 'bookish' vocabulary. Catherine tells Heathcliff that 'I represented your failings in a plain light, *for the purpose of mitigating her adoration*' (X. 90). Thus their speeches do not grip us as soon as they start to speak; they sound rather heavy-footed. Heathcliff's outbursts are too often in the rhetoric of a Byronic hero. The housekeeper's vocabulary is out of character, although it must be remembered that she has read more than people would think, and that Mr Lockwood admits clipping her account.

The skill with which Emily Brontë avoids the monotonous repetition of 'said' in her dialogues is worth noting. For instance, the word occurs only once in Mr Lockwood's conversation with Heathcliff just after he has screamed out in his nightmare (III. 21–23); instead, we find 'called out', 'commenced', 'replied' (twice), 'asked', 'returned', 'hastened to add', 'went on', 'thundered', 'soliloquised', 'muttered'. Three of these words are superior to the word 'said' because they are not only an alternative, but indicate *how* a speech was uttered as well as *what* was said.

The similes and metaphors are sometimes very ordinary, e.g. 'She . . . was off again like a young grey-hound' (XXI. 182), or 'What vain weather-cocks we are!' (IV. 26); sometimes they bear the stamp of genius, e.g. 'A range of gaunt thorns all stretching their limbs one way, as if craving alms of the sun' (I. 2). The similes are usually short, e.g. 'Rough as a saw-edge, and hard as whinstone!' (IV. 28). Later (X. 87) this comparison of Heathcliff with whinstone is used in a metaphor – 'An arid wilderness of furze and whinstone'. Similes and metaphors usually have a connection with the surrounding countryside, and are generally uninviting rather than attractive, e.g.

Good things lost amid a wilderness of weeds, to be sure, whose rankness far overtopped their neglected growth; yet, notwithstanding, evidence of a wealthy soil, that might yield luxuriant crops under other and favourable circumstances.

'I was as reckless as some malefactors show themselves at the foot of the gallows.'

But not always, e.g. 'A voice as sweet as a silver bell' (XXXII. 263).

From *Wuthering Heights* humour, as we usually understand it, is absent. In vain do we look for unspoilt spontaneous laughter. A sense of humour would have helped some of the people in the book to get things into perspective. Such humour as there is breaks grim and saturnine. Joseph's undoubted wit is harshly ironic. The humour of *Wuthering Heights* is a sneering laughter at someone else's expense; laughing *at* people, not *with* them.

Style is difficult to define, and, even when one has listed various qualities in the writing of an author, there may still be something which escapes description, something undoubtedly there, but difficult to detach on its own, like an almond flavour in a cake. It is essential for the student to try to 'feel' the individual character of the style for himself at first hand.

Top Withens

Notes

Chapter I

1801. – Mr Lockwood, new tenant of Thrushcross Grange, tells how he goes to pay a call on his landlord, Mr Heathcliff, of Wuthering Heights. He is received inhospitably, but stops for a while and promises that he will call again on the morrow – an idea not entirely to Heathcliff's satisfaction. Heathcliff's reserve appeals to Mr Lockwood, however – he was reserved himself, indeed, he came to Thrushcross Grange to get away 'from the stir of society', but compared with Heathcliff he feels even sociable.

This chapter contains a description of Heathcliff and of the interior of Wuthering Heights.

WUTHERING, blustering, shaking, tottering (dialect). See text, p.2. The site of the dwelling is assumed to be Top Withens farm, a moorland farm just over three miles from Haworth (see p.9), but Wuthering Heights is much larger than Top Withens. It includes features of Law Hill House, near Halifax, where Emily Brontë taught for a time, a square solid stone house, dour and black in front. A hall she visited from there may have lent other touches.

Thrushcross Grange The site is that of Ponden Hall, about $2\frac{1}{2}$ miles from Haworth, where the Brontës visited, but the Grange of *Wuthering Heights* is a much more splendid establishment.

cattle are the only hedge-cutters i.e. by eating the hedges.

shameless i.e. not ashamed of their nakedness.

date . . . Earnshaw Ponden Hall has a similar inscription. Incidentally, the last date on the inscription above the entrance of Ponden Hall is 1801, the date when Emily makes her story begin. Students who can manage it will find a visit to Haworth and district most rewarding.

penetralium innermost shrine or recess. A humorous use of the word to describe a forbidding farmhouse.

underdrawn shown inadequately.

under-bred pride i.e. pride in being thought one of the ordinary people.

'never told my love' A quotation from Shakespeare's *Twelfth Night* (II. iv. 112).

vis-à-vis opposite (Fr.).

man i.e. servant.

The herd of possessed swine See *Matthew*, VIII. 30–32, *Mark*, V. 11–13, *Luke*, VIII. 30–33. References to the Bible were more commonly understood at the time *Wuthering Heights* was written.

signet i.e. my trade-mark, as we might say, in other words – I should have left the marks of my blow on him.

Chapter II

On his promised return to Wuthering Heights next day, Mr Lockwood is received rudely, even savagely. He is marooned there by a snow-storm, and would have been thrust outside to fend for himself but for the intervention of the housekeeper, after he had been attacked by two dogs. She shows him to a bedroom.

T' For 'the' in the dialect of the West Riding of Yorkshire.

laith barn (dialect).

an if (d.).

flaysome fearful, terrifying, frightful (d.).

Aw'll . . .'t I'll have no hand in it (d.). The West Riding dialect was like a different language in those days.

the door . . . attendance i.e. I had to knock it so loudly.

hemmed i.e. made a 'hem' with my voice.

villain i.e. the pointer bitch.

nowt good for nothing (d.).

postern door leading outside.

copestone i.e. finishing touch. The cope stone is the head stone of a building.

smacked of King Lear Referring to the virulence of King Lear (in Shakespeare's play of that name) towards his favourite daughter, Cordelia, who had piqued him.

housewife i.e. housekeeper.

agait afoot, going on (d.).

Wisht be quiet (d.).

Chapter III

Mr Lockwood spends the night in a room whose window-ledge contains some mildewed books and is scratched with the names *Catherine Earnshaw, Catherine Heathcliff, Catherine Linton*. He reads one of the books which once belonged to Catherine Earnshaw and part of her diary on the spaces in a printed book. He has a wild night in which the names he has read become the people of his dreams. He yells out in his nightmare terror. Heathcliff comes to his room and is greatly affected to find him sleeping in that particular room.

Lockwood dresses, and goes downstairs, filling in the time casually for the next hour – till the household arises at four. He declines breakfast at Wuthering Heights, but Heathcliff accompanies him back to the gates of Thrushcross Grange, two miles from the house itself.

clothes-press A large clothes-cupboard, usually with shelves.

I snuffed it off Old-fashioned candle-wicks did not burn themselves out, but if left became longer as the candle burnt lower and hung down over the candle and burnt with a great smoky flame. Hence they had to be trimmed or 'snuffed', for which 'snuffers' were provided.

lugs ears (d.).

laiking playing (d.).

scroop back cover of a book (d.).

fit finger (d.).

flaysome See note p.38.

gait way (d.). cf. 'agait', note p.38.

laced thrashed (d.).

''owd Nick' i.e. the Devil.

'Seventy Times Seven' See *Matthew*, XVIII. 21–22.

determine into i.e. end in – through neglect.

four hundred and ninety i.e. seventy times seven.

ideal imaginary.

maxillary of the jaw.

Grimalkin A common name for a grey cat. Perhaps the name was suggested by its use in the first scene of Shakespeare's *Macbeth*.

sotto voce in a whisper or an undertone.

snoozled nuzzled (d.).

Revision questions on Chapters I-III

1 Why had Mr Lockwood decided to rent Thrushcross Grange?

2 Give a description of Mr Heathcliff and the farm where he lived.

3 Describe Mr Lockwood's first call at Wuthering Heights. Had you been he, would you have gone again? Give your reasons.

4 Tell in detail Mr Lockwood's nightmare experiences on his second visit to Wuthering Heights.

Chapter IV

Mr Lockwood learns the history of Heathcliff from his housekeeper, Mrs Dean.

He was a foundling brought home from Liverpool by Mr Earnshaw, of Wuthering Heights, to be reared in his own family. Mr Earnshaw and his daughter Catherine took to the boy, but the rest of the family resented his intrusion. The boy bore the blows of Mr Earnshaw's son Hindley and the indifference of others in the household coolly and apparently without vindictiveness, but he knew the hold he had on Mr Earnshaw's heart and made use of it on occasion to get what he wanted. He was a sullen boy and showed neither malice to his persecutors nor gratitude to Mr Earnshaw. He was called 'Heathcliff'.

This chapter contains a description of Heathcliff as a boy.

indigenæ natives (Lat.).

whinstone Hard sandstone.

It's a cuckoo's i.e. he had turned other people out of house and home as a cuckoo turns another bird's eggs out of a nest to make room for her own.

dunnock Hedge-sparrow.

the three kingdoms England, Scotland and Wales.

flighted scolded (d.).

humour temper, mood, disposition, fancy.

Chapter V

Mr Earnshaw began to fail. Hindley was sent to college; at

home, Catherine was always in mischief and was very provocative. She was much too fond of Heathcliff, and he would do her
bidding however she treated him.

The death of Mr Earnshaw came at home, quietly by his
fireside.

The chapter contains a description of Catherine as a girl.

nought good for nothing. cf. the noun ('nowt'), p.38.
as where wherever.
Pharisee i.e. hypocrite.
shopping A misprint (in the L.Y.T. edition) for 'slapping'.
doubt fear.

Chapter VI

Hindley came home to his father's funeral, and brought a wife
with him! She appeared rather a silly girl.

As the new master of the house he lost no time in re-ordering
the *ménage*. Joseph and Mrs Dean were sent to live in the back
kitchen, and Heathcliff was made an outside labourer.
Catherine and Heathcliff slipped out to spend days on the
moors together, thinking it worth the punishment if they should
be found out. One Sunday evening, when they were sent out of
the sitting-room for some trivial offence, they went over the
moors and, getting a glimpse of the lights of Thrushcross
Grange, went to see if the Sunday evenings of the Lintons, who
lived there, were as miserable as those at Wuthering Heights.
Their laughter discovered them as they looked through the
windows; they ran off, but the bulldog caught Catherine by
the ankle and both were taken inside. Heathcliff was sent back
unceremoniously, but Catherine was tenderly looked after.

Hindley was furious at the episode, and told Heathcliff that
dismissal would follow one word spoken to Catherine.

foreigners i.e. strangers. A newcomer to a West Riding village is
  still called a 'foreigner'.
pendent Usually 'pendant'.
Lascar East Indian sailor.
negus A hot mixture of wine and water, flavoured.

Chapter VII

'Catherine stayed at Thrushcross Grange five weeks', and came back on Christmas-eve, looking quite a lady. Heathcliff was abashed at her presence.

The Lintons were invited to spend Christmas-day at Wuthering Heights, as an acknowledgment of what they had done for Catherine. Heathcliff was kept out of the way (at Mrs Linton's request), but on a brief appearance set upon the boy Edgar Linton, who provoked him, and was locked in the garret for the rest of the day. During a dance in the evening Catherine let Heathcliff out, and he sat on a stool by the kitchen fire 'in dumb meditation', 'trying to settle how I shall pay Hindley back. I don't care how long I wait.'

The housekeeper stops her tale and makes as if to go to bed, but Mr Lockwood prays her to go on.

This chapter contains a description of Catherine looking 'like a lady', and of Heathcliff after being left 'uncared for' during her absence (notice the contrast).

habit riding-dress.

mulled heated and mixed with sugar and spices.

cant brisk, merry, cheerful (d.).

donning dressing, preparation.

His cake i.e. Heathcliff's.

for a shower i.e. on account of a shower.

attempting the coxcomb trying to show off.

come The housekeeper's English is not at fault: this is a misprint in the L.Y.T. edition.

the Gimmerton band Students may be reminded of the village band going 'the rounds of all the respectable houses' at Christmas-time, in Thomas Hardy's *Under the Greenwood Tree*. This was in the south of England, which shows how widespread the custom was.

glees part-songs.

my fellow-servant i.e. Joseph.

Chapter VIII

Hindley Earnshaw's wife bore him a son (Hareton), but died of consumption soon afterwards. After her death Hindley became desperate and went to the devil. 'Nobody decent' came near Wuthering Heights, except Edgar Linton. On one of his visits (contrived in the absence of Hindley) he was shocked to see Catherine in a nasty temper, but all the same he found it impossible to leave her.

This chapter contains a portrait of Edgar Linton.

bairn child, lad.
Kenneth The village doctor.
a rush of a lass This phrase probably refers to her thinness, or it may mean 'a lass of no value'.
foster-sister Her mother had been foster-nurse to Hindley (see IV. 29).
hers has been removed See XXIX. 246.
like i.e. a good likeness.
plate metal domestic utensils.
marred spoilt.

Chapter IX

Catherine told Ellen Dean that she had promised to marry Edgar Linton, but with many misgivings, for she knew that she really loved Heathcliff. She was telling Nellie about it when Heathcliff overheard her say that to marry him would degrade her; at that he slipped away, out into a thunder-storm. Catherine went on to the moors to find him, but he had gone for good. She was wet through when she returned, and was dangerously ill with fever. She convalesced at the Grange, but Mr and Mrs Linton both caught the fever and died.

Three years later she married Edgar Linton and went to live at the Grange: Nellie Dean was ordered to accompany her.

bairnies See notes to chapter above.
grat were annoying, vexing, irritating.
mither mother (d.).
mools earth, i.e. of her grave (d.).
clown peasant.
They ... Milo! i.e. people who try and separate us will meet the fate of Milo, a celebrated strong man of ancient Italy who, trying to rend a tree partly split by woodcutters, had his hands caught in the cleft and was eaten up by wolves.
hah isn't how is it that (he) has not? (d.).

nowt See note p.38.

girt eedle seeght! great idle sight (d.).

ill bad.

fahl foul (d.).

war un war worse and worse (d.).

plottered floundered, waded (d.).

Hahsomdiver however (d.).

offald worthless (d.).

Noah and Lot Patriachs of the Old Testament saved by God; Noah from the flood (see *Genesis*, VII. and VIII.), and Lot from Sodom when it was consumed with brimstone and fire (see *Genesis*, XIX. 12–25).

Jonah i.e. the bringer of the storm ('I know that for my sake this great tempest is upon you'. See *Jonah*, I. 3–15).

shoo she (d.).

wer our (d.).

bled her In those days a regular treatment to bring down a fever.

whey The liquid part of milk after curds have formed.

water-gruel i.e. gruel made with water instead of milk.

Revision questions on Chapters IV–IX

1 Old Mr Earnshaw brought Heathcliff home from the best of motives, but do you think that it was a *sensible* thing to do? Give your reasons fully.

2 Describe the character of Catherine as a child.

3 What changes did Hindley make in the household when he became master? Why did Wuthering Heights become such a miserable place to live in?

4 Tell the story of the escapade of Heathcliff and Catherine which led to Catherine's detention at Thrushcross Grange.

5 Describe Catherine's appearance on her return to Wuthering Heights after her convalescence. How did Heathcliff receive her?

6 What sort of a time did Heathcliff have on the following Christmas-day?

7 Give an account of Catherine's conversation with Ellen Dean on the evening of the day she had accepted Edgar Linton. What does it show of her character?

Chapter X

Mr Lockwood is ill after his experience at Wuthering Heights, and it is four weeks before he is able to listen to the rest of the story.

One September night at dusk, after Catherine and Edgar had been married 'half a year', Mrs Dean was startled to find Heathcliff in the shadows at Thrushcross Grange. Catherine was 'too excited to show gladness'. Heathcliff was invited into the parlour with her husband's unwilling consent. He had grown tall, athletic and upright, and looked quite a gentleman. He stopped an hour or so, and during his stay Catherine was beside herself with joy. He left for Wuthering Heights, where, he said, he had been invited to stay by Hindley.

He visited Thrushcross Grange from time to time, cautiously at first and regularly later on, and walked on the moors with Catherine (and Edgar's sister Isabella). By Joseph's account he was spending his time at Wuthering Heights winning Hindley's money from him at dice. But Edgar now found new trouble. His sister was greatly attracted by Heathcliff, and she admitted as much to Catherine. Very maliciously Catherine told Heathcliff of Isabella's infatuation for him in front of her, in exaggerated terms. Heathcliff, however, seemed uninterested.

This chapter contains a description of Heathcliff on his return and of Isabella at the age of eighteen, and Catherine's estimate of Heathcliff's character to Isabella.

Kenneth See note p.43.

leeches Used by doctors to bleed people. See note on 'bled her', p.44. The word thus came to be used for the doctors themselves.

sizar A student accepted at a cheap rate at Cambridge in return for doing certain chores.

earn honours ... foster-country The War of American Independence lasted from 1775 to 1783.

sough A furrow in the earth for draining off water.

that creature i.e. her husband.

whinstone See note p.40.

crahnr's 'quest enah coroner's inquest enough (d.).

grand 'sizes grand assizes, i.e. the day of the last judgment (d.).

girn show his teeth in, growl, snarl.

Broad road i.e. to destruction. cf. the title of the Sunday night book (III. 17), 'T' Broad Way to Destruction'.

pikes turnpikes. The sense is, 'to make his way easy'.

justice-meeting i.e. meeting of the justices of the peace, magistrates.

he returned A bad misprint for 'she' in the L.Y.T. edition.

Chapter XI

Passing the gate at Wuthering Heights one day, Nellie Dean found it obvious that little Hareton was being brought up like a savage.

The next time Heathcliff came to Thrushcross Grange he made advances to Isabella, and admitted to Catherine that it was out of revenge (but not, he said, revenge against her). Edgar turned him out of the house, in an episode where Edgar was made to appear a 'milk-blooded coward'. After that was done Catherine put on an act, and there followed another violent scene – between Catherine and her husband. Edgar told Isabella that he would disown her if she encouraged Heathcliff.

the farm i.e. Wuthering Heights.

warn him i.e. Hindley.

sand-pillar i.e. pillar of sandstone.

guide-post sign-post.

my young lady i.e. Isabella.

after sending to send.

lay forget, put aside.

Chapter XII

Catherine's angry petulance and fierce temper made her really ill, and brought on a fit of delirium.

On a moonless winter's night Isabella ran off with Heathcliff into the 'misty darkness'.

water . . . decanter i.e. washing water and drinking water.

they put pigeons' . . . die There were several country superstitions about pigeons, because they are so indigestible, and, therefore, the cause of stomach disorders. Pigeons were a regular winter food of country gentlemen in those days, when the alternative was salted meat.

moor-cock Red grouse.

lapwing Plover.

swells Undulating ridges (of the heath or moorland).

elf-bolts Bolts (or arrows) shot by fairies.

press See note on 'clothes-press', p.39.

the oak-panelled bed See III. 15.

you go . . . me! i.e. when you are buried.

bridle hook i.e. to which to tie a horse.

springer A kind of spaniel (strictly speaking, one used to 'spring' game).

Chapter XIII

Two months later Catherine was better, but still weak after brain fever.

Isabella, now married to Heathcliff, told Ellen Dean in a letter how miserable beyond words she was at Wuthering Heights, and asked her to tell Edgar that she would like to see him, but not to mention any details of her distress.

ganging going (d.).

say see.

mud must.

thible A stick for stirring the contents of a cooking-pot (d.).

nave fist (d.).

pale skim (d.).

guilp pot (d.).

deaved knocked, broken violently (d.).

meeterly clane clean enough, fairly clean (d.).

mells on't meddles with it (d.).

valances Short curtains round a bedstead.

marred See note p.43.

Miss Cathy! i.e. with a temper like Miss Cathy's.

madling fool, simpleton, blockhead (d.).

plisky rage (d.).

Chapter XIV

Edgar sent a message back to Isabella by Ellen that there could be no communication between the two households.

Ellen found Isabella looking a listless slut – her hand had subdued itself to what it worked in. Heathcliff admitted that they hated one another. Isabella now knew that he had married her to obtain power over Edgar. She was kept a prisoner.

Heathcliff told Ellen that he had been lurking round the Grange gardens waiting for an opportunity to see Catherine. Ellen said that she would inform her master, whereupon he threatened to have her locked up in Wuthering Heights till the next morning, while he saw Catherine, by force if necessary.

In the long run Ellen was half persuaded, half compelled to take a letter to Catherine, and, if she consented to see Heathcliff, to inform him of Linton's next absence from home.

the person . . . necessity i.e. Edgar.
At a most miserable . . . kind See IX. 68.
Hercules A hero of prodigious strength in classical mythology, who performed twelve 'labours' (heroic feats of strength and valour).
brach bitch.
dree long, slow, tedious (d.).

Chapter XV

Ellen decided not to give Heathcliff's letter to Catherine until her husband was out, which was the next Sunday. Heathcliff had been hanging round the Grange, however, and, when he saw for himself that Linton had gone to church, he came in of his own accord – about the same time as Catherine received his letter. Catherine and he were lost in one another, but she seemed a far away, unearthly creature. Heathcliff said that he forgave *his* murderer (Cathy) but could not forgive hers (Linton). After service time Heathcliff tried to go, but Catherine would not loose him, even when Linton approached the door. And when Linton came into the room, Heathcliff handed to him Catherine's lifeless-looking form. In his anxiety for Catherine, Edgar forgot all about Heathcliff, who slipped out into the garden.

This chapter contains a description of Catherine between her last illness and her death.

teased handled roughly. The word was stronger in meaning than now.

humour See note p.40.

Chapter XVI

Catherine died quietly that night, two hours after the birth of a puny daughter (the Cathy whom Mr Lockwood saw at Wuthering Heights). She lay beautiful in death.

Mrs Dean went out to tell Heathcliff the news, but he had sensed it. In selfish passion he cursed the one he claimed to love ('May she wake in torment!') and howled that he could not live without her – his life, his soul.

Catherine's husband was the only family mourner at the funeral. She was buried under a simple headstone in the open.

you saw at Wuthering Heights See Chapter II.

securing . . . son's Old Mr Linton left his estate to Edgar and his sons (but not his daughters) ; failing Edgar's having male issue it went to his own daughter (Isabella) and her son(s).

ousels Small birds of the thrush family, not unlike blackbirds, with a white crescent on their breasts. They are moorland birds.

The place of Catherine's interment As she wished (see XII. 109).

Chapter XVII

After shocking scenes at Wuthering Heights, Isabella took the opportunity to escape to Thrushcross Grange. She would not stay, nor allow Edgar to be told of her visit, but left after an hour to go south, near London, where a son (Linton) was born to her in a few months. She never revisited her home country again, although she corresponded with Edgar.

Hindley Earnshaw died some six months later, and Heathcliff became the new owner of Wuthering Heights, as Hindley had mortgaged his land to Heathcliff to pay his gaming debts.

Heathcliff intimated that if Mr Linton tried to remove Hareton from Wuthering Heights he would get Isabella's child to take his place.

This chapter contains a description of Isabella after running away from Wuthering Heights (the last we see of her).

doll of a child i.e. small child.
Methodist Follower of John Wesley, whose evangelical movement had started about forty years before this.
't' little maister' Hareton.
the click of my snuffers See note on 'I snuffed it off', p.39.
'girned' See note p.■■.
preterhuman beyond human.
it is i.e. 'that stuff' – Earnshaw's blood – is.
I was . . . gallows This was in the days of public hanging.
Fanny Isabella's dog at the Grange (see XII. 110).
she should not . . . himself It would interfere with his revenge against Linton if the presence of his sister made him happy.
foster-brother See note on 'foster-sister', p.43.
tent care (d.).

Revision questions on Chapters X-XVII

1 Describe the way in which Heathcliff came back to Thrushcross Grange after his three years' absence from the neighbourhood. How did his return affect Catherine?

2 What character did Catherine give Heathcliff to Isabella?

3 Describe Isabella's elopement with Heathcliff. Why did he want to marry her?

4 Describe the scene where Edgar Linton had Heathcliff turned out of his house. What effect had this on Catherine?

5 Give an account of the contents of Isabella's letter to Ellen Dean.

6 Describe the events of the Sunday evening when Heathcliff called at Thrushcross Grange during Edgar's absence at church.

7 After she had run away, what did Isabella tell Ellen Dean of her experiences at Wuthering Heights? Describe her appearance when she burst into the parlour at Thrushcross Grange.

8 How did Catherine's death affect Heathcliff (immediately afterwards, not in the years succeeding)?

Chapter XVIII
The story misses twelve years. Cathy was now thirteen, and had an irresistible desire to go to Peniston Crags, which her father had forbidden (as the way lay past Wuthering Heights). She tricked Mrs Dean and slipped off there in her father's absence from home (upon Isabella's last illness and death), and was found by Ellen late in the day at Wuthering Heights. Fortunately Heathcliff was out. Hareton had met her and been with her to the Crags. She was disgusted to be told that Hareton, whom she took for a servant, was her cousin!

Cathy made a promise to Mrs Dean not to tell her father that she had been to Wuthering Heights – and kept it.

This chapter contains a description of Cathy at thirteen and of Hareton at eighteen.

heath i.e. heather.

Penistone Misprint for 'Peniston' in the L.Y.T. edition – continued throughout the chapter. (Conversely, Mrs Dean sometimes has an *e* added to her name.) The name was no doubt suggested to Emily Brontë by a quarry only a few minutes' walk from the parsonage called 'Penistone Quarry'.

pointers Game dogs. On scenting game they stand still and point their muzzles towards it.

Galloway A small horse (of a breed from Galloway, Scotland).

from the Grange i.e. from the boundary of the park.

goblin-hunter Presumably the will-o'-the-wisp.

fairishes fairies.

clown See note p.43.

wisht See note p.38.

'offalld' See note p.44.

Chapter XIX
After Isabella's funeral Edgar brought home her boy, a peevish, delicate child. That same night Heathcliff sent Joseph across for his lad – 'and Aw munn't goa back 'bout him'.

Edgar refused to have the boy woken up for further travel, but said that he should come in the morning.

This chapter contains a description of Isabella's boy, Linton Heathcliff, at nearly thirteen years of age.

'bout without.

Chapter XX

Early next morning Ellen was told to take little Linton to Wuthering Heights (to forestall Heathcliff's arrival to fetch him). The boy could not understand this new development, had never heard of his father, and was reluctant to go.

Heathcliff sneered at 'The whey-faced whining wretch', but said that he would look after him well – after all (in the absence of any other male heir) he was the prospective owner of Thrushcross Grange! The poor child was scared of staying at Wuthering Heights, but nothing could be done.

Chapter XXI

On her sixteenth birthday Cathy, with Ellen, met Heathcliff on the moor. He invited them inside Wuthering Heights, Ellen protesting at Cathy's acceptance of the invitation. Cathy thus found out that her cousin Linton, who disappeared so mysteriously, had been but four miles away all the time. She failed to understand how relatives living so near one another could wish to keep apart. Heathcliff desired the boy and girl to fall in love, so that there would be no dispute that they would be joint successors to the lands of the two families.

When Cathy got back to the Grange her father forbade further visits to Wuthering Heights. Weeks afterwards Ellen discovered that she had been conducting a clandestine correspondence with Linton. She burnt her love-letters before her eyes under penalty of showing them to her father, and stopped the correspondence forthwith.

This chapter contains a description of Cathy at sixteen years of age, and of Linton a little younger.

nab short, steep, rocky hill.
Penistone See note p.51.
elastic as steel The author is thinking of the steel of a sword.
'gaumless' 'stupid', half-witted.
extra-animal outside our animal nature.

Chapter XXII

On a walk with Ellen one day in late autumn Cathy lost her hat over the wall of the park. She clambered down into the road to retrieve it and was unable to get back for some time. Meanwhile who should come along but Heathcliff! He told Cathy that Linton was in love with her 'in earnest', and was literally dying for her. He said that he was going to be away from home for the rest of the week. Would she call and see Linton? A visit from her would save him.

Michaelmas 29 September (the Feast of St Michael).
starved perished with cold.
sackless feeble, helpless (d.).
canty See note on 'cant', p.42.
a Slough of Despond i.e. utter despair. From Bunyan's *Pilgrim's Progress*, where one of Christian's trials to get across this slough.
idiotcy 'Idiocy', of course, is the word, and the one Emily Brontë used. The misprint is repeated in Chapter XXVII. (L.Y.T. edition).

Chapter XXIII

Accompanied by Ellen, Cathy went to Wuthering Heights next morning. It was obvious that once the master was away Linton was neglected. However, he made the most of his illness to get attention. Cathy and Linton flared up into a quarrel about the love affairs of their mothers and fathers. Ellen was now laid up for three weeks, through sitting with wet feet for so long at Wuthering Heights.

elysium In Greek mythology the abode of the blessed after death, hence a state of ideal happiness.
'But you've ... passion' Spoken by Mrs Dean.

Chapter XXIV

When she was better, Ellen found out that while she had been ill Cathy had gone every night after tea to Wuthering Heights. The girl admitted that, on the whole, the evenings there were 'dreary and troubled'. Ellen passed on the information to her master, and Cathy's visits were forbidden.

Michael The groom.
he looked ... above See I. 2.

sarve ye eht serve you out, i.e. give you what you deserve, get his
own back (d.).

skift shift (d.).

Chapter XXV

Mr Linton was declining, and eventually was won over to
consider young Linton as a suitor for his daughter by 'a natural
desire that she might retain – or at least return in a short time
to – the house of her ancestors; and he considered her only
prospect of doing that was by a union with his heir'. He agreed
to Cathy and Linton having a ride or a walk together about
once a week, under Ellen's guardianship.

Chapter XXVI

On their first such weekly meeting, it was obvious that Linton
was terrorised by his father into meeting Cathy.

gang See note on 'ganging', p.47.

nab See note p.52.

ongoings A compound for 'goings on'. There used to be more
variation in the position of prefixes and suffixes formerly than now
(e.g. 'my downsitting and my uprising'), but this form is surprising
for an educated person as late as the (supposed) end of the eighteenth
century.

Chapter XXVII

On their second meeting with Linton, Cathy and Ellen were
tricked into entering Wuthering Heights, and Heathcliff locked
them in. He said that they would not be set free until Cathy
and Linton were married. Ellen was imprisoned with Cathy
the first night, and in a room by herself for four days and nights
more.

at your service i.e. (contempt) for you.

cockatrice Reptile (actually a fabulous one).

eft Newt.

Chapter XXVIII

Linton and Cathy were married perforce, and at the last
minute death prevented Mr Linton's leaving Cathy's fortune

in trust, as he had intended. Cathy escaped from Wuthering Heights just in time to see her father before he died.

winked shut my eyes (not merely one eye).

Revision questions on Chapters XVIII-XXVIII

1 Describe Cathy's first venture 'beyond the range of the park by herself'.

2 Tell of Linton's arrival at Thrushcross Grange and Joseph's call for him the same night.

3 Describe Heathcliff's first meeting with his son.

4 Give an account of Cathy's outing on the sixteenth anniversary of her birthday.

5 Write a pen-portrait of Cathy and of Linton at about sixteen years of age.

6 What aroused Ellen Dean's suspicions that Cathy and Linton were secretly exchanging letters? Do you think that the action she took was right?

7 Describe Cathy's unexpected meeting with Heathcliff on the road over the park wall. What were its consequences?

8 How did Ellen Dean discover that Cathy had been making nightly rides to Wuthering Heights? What action did she take on this occasion?

9 By what trick were Ellen and Cathy made prisoners in Wuthering Heights, and with what purpose? How was Cathy eventually able to escape?

10 Give an account of a meeting between Cathy and Linton not described in any other answer on these chapters, and say what it reveals of their characters.

Chapter XXIX

Heathcliff became the new owner of Thrushcross Grange. The evening after Mr Linton's funeral he packed Cathy off to Wuthering Heights and resolved to let the Grange.

He told Ellen Dean that he would take Catherine's portrait

home. He went on to describe how he had felt the presence of
Catherine haunting him through all the long years since her
death, and said that when the sexton was digging Mr Linton's
grave he opened Catherine's grave and 'saw her face again'.

Chapter XXX

Linton died, leaving all his movable property to his father.
The Grange lands he could not meddle with, as a minor, but
Heathcliff 'claimed and kept them in his wife's right and his
also'.

Cathy was ill for a fortnight after Linton's death.

Mrs Dean ends her story with a description of Cathy's miserable life at Wuthering Heights, and her haughty and reserved
nature. 'I despise you, and will have nothing to say to any of
you!' were her words to Hareton.

'thrang' busy (d.).
Methodists See note p.50.
Baptists Members of a religious body who object to infant baptism
and practise baptism by immersion on people who are old enough to
understand the symbolism of the act.
starved See note p.53.
stalled of sickened with (d.). the equivalent of 'fed up with'.
wake stop up, keep awake.

Chapter XXXI

Mr Lockwood (now nearly recovered) goes to Wuthering
Heights to tell Heathcliff that he will not be renewing his lease
of Thrushcross Grange beyond the twelve months originally
agreed. (He is going to London at once.) Heathcliff is out, and
before his return he sees evidence of Cathy's cheerless life,
against which she subconsciously rebels with a spiteful tongue.

dinner-time i.e. noon.
stalled See notes to chapter above.
Chevy Chase One of the oldest of English ballads.

Chapter XXXII

The following September, on a journey north, Mr Lockwood
turns aside to revisit Gimmerton, arrives unexpectedly at the

Grange and finds a new housekeeper in residence. Mrs Dean has gone to be housekeeper at Wuthering Heights.

He makes his way there. Through the window he sees Cathy happily giving Hareton a reading lesson. Inside, he hears from Mrs Dean that Heathcliff has been dead three months and that Cathy and Hareton are more than friends.

This chapter contains a description of Cathy at eighteen and of Hareton at twenty-three.

devastate the moors i.e. have a shooting holiday.

swells See note p.47.

norther neither.

mensful tidy, clean, decent (d.).

lugs See note p.39.

hahsiver however (d.). cf. 'hahsomdiver', note p.44.

shoo See note p.44.

witched bewitched (d).

wer See note p.44.

rullers rulers (d).

fellies fellows (d.).

jocks provisions, supplies (d.). A 'jockshop' in West Riding dialect was a common eating-house.

shaamed was put to shame (d.).

reaming foaming (hence 'silver').

Juno One of the dogs (see II. 7).

he became i.e. Earnshaw.

gait See note p.39.

shoon The old plural of 'shoe'.

mitch much (d.).

Chapter XXXIII

Mr Lockwood hears from Ellen how on one occasion during Heathcliff's lifetime Cathy persuaded Hareton to clear some currant and gooseberry bushes to make way for flowers. These currant bushes were 'the apple of Joseph's eye', and when he discovered their loss he pretended to give notice. Heathcliff was furious, but Cathy's tongue, supplemented by Hareton in unexpected alliance with her, caused him to desist from hurting her, and also, he admitted later to Mrs Dean, he felt a certain lethargy sapping his power of action.

This chapter contains a comparison of the appearance of Cathy and of Hareton with Catherine.

an ye will For 'an' see note p.38.

stale, steal (d.).

bud whet but what (d.).

witched See note p.57.

on of (d.).

riven pulled.

the day . . . Crags See Chapter XVIII.

Hercules See note p.48.

monomania madness concerning one subject.

Chapter XXXIV

Heathcliff died in the early summer, after strange and unnerving behaviour, in which he looked ghastly yet seemed thrilled by a wild inner joy. 'My soul's bliss kills my body, but does not satisfy itself.' Everyone shrank from him. Only two people attended his funeral, and one of those merely from a sense of duty. The doctor 'was perplexed to pronounce of what disorder' he died.

Hareton and Cathy, Mr Lockwood is told, are to be married on New Year's Day and will live at the Grange.

On his return Mr Lockwood goes out of his way to look at the three head-stones in the kirkyard – Catherine's in the middle, Edgar Linton's on one side and Heathcliff's on the other. He lingers round them in the peace of the evening and wonders 'how anyone could ever imagine unquiet slumbers for the sleepers in that quiet earth'.

who had . . . accident See Chapter XXXII.

that with the panelled bed i.e. Catherine's old room. See Chapter III.

harboured . . . bane i.e. harboured by old Mr Earnshaw and leading to the destruction of his family.

basin of coffee In those days tea and coffee were often served in basins or dishes.

Green The local lawyer. See Chapter XXVIII.

Titan In Greek mythology one of a race of giant men (or gods) of
tremendous strength.

space i.e. time.

my directions concerning the two coffins See Chapter XXIX.

they refused . . . Kirk A suicide could not be buried in consecrated
ground.

chuck A term of endearment, e.g. 'my pretty one'.

panels i.e. of the bed.

grumbled Because he felt that he must go.

the middle one i.e. Catherine's. The height of the turf and moss up
the head-stones shows how long it is since each has been laid.

heath See note p.51.

Revision questions on Chapters XXIX-XXXIV

1 How did Heathcliff get possession of (a) Wuthering Heights,
(b) Thrushcross Grange?

2 'Is he a ghoul or a vampire?' Mention anything ghoulish
that is related of Heathcliff in these chapters.

3 Trace the growth of affection between Cathy and Hareton.

4 Give examples of Heathcliff's cruelty to Cathy.

5 What changes did Mr Lockwood find when he came back to
Gimmerton in September 1802?

6 What were the consequences of the 'devastation' of Joseph's
currant and gooseberry bushes by Cathy and Hareton?

7 Compare the appearance of Cathy and of Hareton with that
of Catherine.

8 Give instances of Heathcliff's unnatural behaviour during
the month or two before his death.

9 Describe the death of Heathcliff.

10 Do you think that Cathy and Hareton have good prospects
of happiness (as distinct from prosperity)?

Questions

General questions

1 Discuss the relationship of *Wuthering Heights* (including any of the characters therein) to the personal life and environment of Emily Brontë.

2 In what parts of the plot does Emily Brontë use (a) a diary, (b) a letter, (c) a chance conversation in the street or on the moors, to tell her story?

3 'The construction of *Wuthering Heights* is often regarded as its weakest point. It has been called "clumsy" by more than one critic'. p.4). Say what may have prompted this criticism, and consider what can be said in praise of the structure of the novel.

4 Give examples of Emily Brontë's exactness in details of time and place. What is the effect of this on the reader?

5 Mention is made on page 11 of 'the improbabilities and co-incidences . . . of *Wuthering Heights*'. Give an account of one important improbability and one important coincidence, stating whether the instances chosen detract from your enjoyment of the novel.

6 Do you consider the marriage of Hareton and Cathy to be an anticlimax? Give your reasons.

7 'A prevailing intensity is characteristic of *Wuthering Heights*.' Discuss and illustrate this criticism.

8 *Wuthering Heights* has often been called a 'depressing' book. Say what characteristics of the novel may have suggested this adjective, and consider how far you think it can truthfully be applied.

9 'The action is laid in hell, only it seems places and people have English names there.' Comment on this fierce judgment of *Wuthering Heights*.

10 How far was Heathcliff 'more sinned against than sinning'?

11 To what extent does Heathcliff's character *develop*, and to what extent is the man the same as the boy?

12 Analyse the way love and a desire for revenge influence Heathcliff after the marriage of Catherine.

13 What do we learn of the character of Heathcliff from the way he treats Isabella?

14 'He declares to Mrs Dean that he never harmed anybody – they all brought their ruin upon themselves' (p.13). Is Heathcliff justified in thus relieving himself of responsibility for his misdeeds?

15 Would you say that Catherine loved herself more than she loved Heathcliff or Edgar? Give your reasons.

16 Do you think that Catherine had less or more influence over Heathcliff dead than alive?

17 Would you call Cathy Linton an attractive character? Illustrate your answer fully.

18 Give an account of one time when (a) Catherine, (b) her daughter Cathy was 'in a pet', and compare and contrast them in full.

19 In what ways was (a) Edgar a typical Linton, (b) Hareton a typical Earnshaw?

20 Write a character-sketch of Joseph.

21 Mrs Dean plays a large part in the story. Show its importance, and mention any occasions where her character has a tranquilising influence.

22 Which of the characters in *Wuthering Heights* most excites your (a) pity, (b) admiration? Refer to incidents in the novel to support your choice.

23 'There is no character in *Wuthering Heights* who is completely lovable. . . . Neither is there any character who is completely odious.' What is your opinion? Illustrate fully.

24 *Wuthering Heights* 'tells of the incredible deeds of incredible people'. How far do you agree with this sweeping statement?

25 Give examples of contrast in *Wuthering Heights* (including character-contrast).

26 Give a short account of two episodes in the story which reveal (a) suspense, (b) humour, (c) pathos.

27 Mention any episode in *Wuthering Heights* which you felt that you must read a second time, and say why.

28 Discuss the merits and demerits of Emily Brontë's prose style.

29 *Wuthering Heights* is one of the most popular novels in English fiction. Try to account for this.

30 Compare and contrast Emily Brontë as a novelist with her sister Charlotte, using *Wuthering Heights* and *Jane Eyre* for reference.

Context questions

Answer briefly the questions below each of the following passages.

1 'You've made me afraid and ashamed of you', he continued; 'I'll not come here again!'

Her eyes began to glisten, and her lids to twinkle.

'And you told me a deliberate untruth!' he said.

'I didn't!' she cried, recovering her speech; 'I did nothing deliberately. Well go, if you please – get away! And now I'll cry – I'll cry myself sick!'

She dropped down on her knees by a chair, and set to weeping in serious earnest.

a) Why was he 'afraid' and 'ashamed' of her?

b) What was the 'deliberate untruth' of which she was accused?

c) State the immediate cause of this quarrel.

d) 'He' was soon back again. What occasioned his change of mind?

2 'I was not aware there were eavesdroppers,' muttered the detected villain. 'Worthy Mrs Dean I like you, but I don't like your double-dealing,' he added aloud. 'How could *you* lie so glaringly, as to affirm I hated the "poor child"? and invent bugbear stories to terrify her from my door-stones? Catherine Linton (the very name warms me), my bonnie lass, I shall be from home all this week; go and see if I have not spoken truth.'

a) Where was Mrs Dean 'eavesdropping'? What occasioned her to be away from Cathy?

b) How was her presence revealed?

c) Give the substance of the conversation to which she was listening.

d) Who was 'the "poor child"'?

e) Had Heathcliff 'spoken truth'?

f) Did Cathy 'go and see' for herself?

g) Do you think that Mrs Dean was ever guilty of double-dealing?

h) Would you call *Wuthering Heights* a 'bugbear story'?

3 Inform Edgar that I'd give the world to see his face again – that my heart returned to Thrushcross Grange in twenty-four hours after I left it, and is there at this moment, full of warm feelings for him, and Catherine! *I can't follow it, though* – (those words are underlined) they need not expect me, and they may draw what conclusions they please; taking care, however, to lay nothing at the door of my weak will or deficient affection.

The remainder of the letter is for yourself alone. I want to ask you two questions: the first is – How did you contrive to preserve the common sympathies of human nature when you resided here? . . .

The second question, I have great interest in; it is this – Is Mr Heathcliff a man? If so, is he mad? And if not, is he a devil? I shan't tell my reasons for making this inquiry; but, I beseech you to explain, if you can, what I have married: that is, when you call to see me; and you must call, Ellen, very soon. Don't write, but come, and bring me something from Edgar.

a) Where was this letter written?
b) Is there any mention in the story of any other letter written by the same person?
c) Why could not the writer follow her heart? What does she imply without specifically stating it?
d) What would you say are the answers to the two questions?
e) Did Ellen come to see her?

4 ' "They have let the bull-dog loose, and he holds me!" The devil had seized her ankle, Nellie: I heard his abominable snorting. She did not yell out – no! she would have scorned to do it, if she had been spitted on the horns of a mad cow. I did, though!'

a) Who were 'they'?
b) Whereabouts did this happen?
c) 'I did, though!' What did *he* yell?
d) What was (i) the immediate, and (ii) the lasting effect of this incident?
e) On what day of the week did it happen?

5 That Friday made the last of our fine days for a month. In the evening, the weather broke: the wind shifted from south to north-east, and brought rain first, and then sleet and snow. On the morrow one could hardly imagine that there had been three weeks of summer.

a) 'That Friday.' Which Friday?

b) What particular signs that 'three weeks of summer' had gone back to winter are mentioned later in this description?

c) Point out the sympathetic background.

d) At what part of the chapter does this description occur? Have you any comment to make on this?

6 'What do you mean?' asked Zillah. 'It's not his tale: they tell that in the village – about your being lost in the marsh: and I calls to Earnshaw, when I come in – "Eh, they's queer things, Mr Hareton, happened since I went off. It's a sad pity of that likely young lass, and cant Nellie Dean." He stared. I thought he had not heard aught, so I told him the rumour. The master listened, and he just smiled to himself!'

a) What was (i) the rumour, (ii) the true story?

b) Why should the master 'smile to himself'?

c) Who was Zillah?

d) What instruction did she receive from the master immediately following this?

7 One of the maids mentioning the Fairy Cave, quite turned her head with a desire to fulfil this project: she teased Mr Linton about it; and he promised she should have the journey when she got older. But Miss Catherine measured her age by months, and, 'Now, am I old enough to go to Peniston Crags?' was the constant question in her mouth.

a) Where were the Fairy Cave and Peniston Crags?

b) 'This project'. Which project?

c) Why did Mr Linton not want Catherine to go to Peniston Crags?

d) When did she first go to Peniston Crags? In whose company? Briefly describe the sequel to the incident.

8 'It's noan Nellie!' answered Joseph. 'Aw sudn't shift fur Nellie – nasty ill nowt as shoo is. Thank God! *shoo* cannot stale t' sowl o' nob'dy! Shoo wer niver soa handsome, bud whet a body mud look at her 'baht winking. It's yon flaysome, graceless quean, ut's witched ahr lad, wi' her bold een un' her forrard ways – till – Nay! it fair brusts my heart! He's forgotten all Ee done for him, un' made on him, un' goan un' riven up a whole row ut t' grandest currant trees i' t' garden!' And here he lamented outright; unmanned by a sense of his bitter injuries, and Earnshaw's ingratitude and dangerous condition.

a) Render this dialect speech in Queen's English.
b) To whom in particular was it spoken?
c) What was the occasion of this outburst?
d) What was it intended to set in place of the currant trees?
e) At what time of year did this occur?

9 Mr Earnshaw, the old master, came downstairs, dressed for a journey; and after he had told Joseph what was to be done during the day, he turned to Hindley, and Cathy, and me – for I sat eating my porridge with them – and he said, speaking to his son, 'Now my bonny man, I'm going to Liverpool today, what shall I bring you? You may choose what you like: only let it be little, for I shall walk there and back.'

a) What did Hindley and Cathy choose as presents?
b) How far was it to Liverpool?
c) How long did it take Mr Earnshaw to make the journey there and back?
d) What time at night did he return?
e) Did the children get their promised presents?

10 Mr Heathcliff, meeting me one day in the village, inquired where she lived. I refused to tell. He remarked that it was not of any moment, only she must beware of coming to her brother: she should not be with him, if he had to keep her himself. Though I would give no information, he discovered, through some of the other servants, both her place of residence and the existence of the child. Still he didn't molest her: for which forbearance she might thank his aversion, I suppose. He often asked about the infant, when he saw me; and on hearing its name, smiled grimly, and observed:

'They wish me to hate it too, do they?'

'I don't think they wish you to know anything about it,' I answered.

'But I'll have it,' he said, 'when I want it. They may reckon on that!'

a) Where was Isabella living?

b) What was Heathcliff's objection to her living with her brother?

c) What sort of a creature did Isabella report her child to be?

d) 'I'll have it . . . when I want it.' When did he carry out his threat?

11 A sudden impulse seized me to visit Thrushcross Grange. It was scarcely noon, and I conceived that I might as well pass the night under my own roof as in an inn. Besides, I could spare a day easily to arrange matters with my landlord, and thus save myself the trouble of invading the neighbourhood again. Having rested a while, I directed my servant to inquire the way to the village; and, with great fatigue to our beasts, we managed the distance in some three hours.

a) Where was the speaker at the time?

b) Where was he going?

c) What month and year was it?

d) 'In some three hours.' How far was it?

e) What changes did he find at Thrushcross Grange when he arrived there?

12 'No,' she added after a while; 'I cannot sit in the kitchen. Set two tables here, Ellen: one for your master and Miss Isabella, being gentry; the other for Heathcliff and myself, being of the lower orders. Will that please you, dear? Or must I have a fire lighted elsewhere? If so, give directions. I'll run down and secure my guest. I'm afraid the joy is too great to be real!'

a) Where was the guest?

b) Who first saw Heathcliff?

c) At that time of year was it and on what sort of an evening?

d) What made Catherine refer to the kitchen?

e) What word did Edgar use to describe Catherine's sarcastic suggestions?

f) When Heathcliff left, where was he bound?

13 I gave Michael books and pictures to prepare Minny every evening, and to put her back in the stable: you mustn't scold *him* either, mind. I was at the Heights by half-past six, and generally stayed till half-past eight, and then galloped home. It was not to amuse myself that I went: I was often wretched all the time.

a) Who was Michael?

b) 'You mustn't scold *him* either, mind.' What does this show about Cathy's character?

c) 'It was not to amuse myself that I went: I was often wretched all the time.' Why, then, did she go?

d) Briefly tell what happened on one of these excursions.

e) How was Cathy's deception found out?

14 We heard him mount the stairs directly: he did not proceed to his ordinary chamber, but turned into that with the panelled bed: its window, as I mentioned before, is wide enough for anybody to get through; and it struck me that he plotted another midnight excursion, of which he had rather we had no suspicion.

a) Describe the 'panelled bed'.

b) Whose was it aforetime?

c) Where else in *Wuthering Heights* is it mentioned and in what connection?

d) What made it easy for anyone to get through that particular window?

e) What did Mrs Dean think was Heathcliff's reason for not proceeding 'to his ordinary chamber'?

15 'It is hard to forgive, and to look at those eyes, and feel those wasted hands,' he answered. 'Kiss me again; and don't let me see your eyes! I forgive what you have done to me. I love *my* murderer – but *yours*! How can I?'

They were silent – their faces hid against each other, and washed by each other's tears.

a) Mention any other place in the story where 'those eyes' are referred to.

b) Whom does he mean by (i) '*my* murderer', (ii) *yours*?

c) ' "How can I?" ' Did he?

d) Are you surprised that *both* were crying?

e) What day of the week did this conversation take place and at what time? Explain the circumstances briefly.

Key to context questions

1 VIII. 60; **2** XXII. 200; **3** XIII. 116; **4** VI. 40; **5** XVII. 145; **6** XXVIII. 238; **7** XVIII. 163; **8** XXXIII. 273; **9** IV. 29; **10** XVII. 156–157; **11** XXXII. 261; **12** X. 80; **13** XXIV. 211; **14** XXXIV. 282; **15** XV. 138.